The New Story of Trull

Trull church in 1860

The New Story of Trull

Researched and Written by the
Trull Parish Archive Group
Edited by Don Archer

HARRY GALLOWAY PUBLISHING

The modern photographs on pages 47, 101, 118, 123, 128, 129, 130 and 132 were taken by Don Archer; on pages 39, 40, 44, 46, 66, 73, 74, 76, 78, 80, 82, 85, 87, 89, 90, 108, 118, 120, 121, 131 and 145 by Graham Grant; on pages 13, 14, 16-19, 21-25, 27 and 28 by Mark McDermott. The drawings of All Saints church on page 37 and the Old Village Hall on page 124 are by Neville Cox and Mark Pritchard respectively.

The cover photograph was taken by Graham Grant.

All rights reserved. No part of this publication may be reproduced, stored in a retrieval system or transmitted in any form or by any means, electronic, mechanical, photocopying, recording or otherwise, without the prior written permission of the publisher and copyright holder. Every care has been taken to check the accuracy of the information contained in this book. Neither the publisher nor the author are responsible for any consequences arising from the use of the information contained herein. Exclusive permission has been obtained from the individuals quoted to publish their memories.

The book was researched and written by the Trull Parish Archive Group, consisting of Don Archer, Graham Grant and Mark McDermott, based at the Trull Church Community Centre, Church Road, Trull, Taunton, TA3 7JZ. The original *The Story of Trull* was compiled by members of Trull & Staplehay Women's Institute, edited by Olive Hallam and published in 1953.

***The New Story of Trull* is dedicated to the memory of**
Cyril Green
the doyen of Trull historians

Set in Garamond.
All correspondence to the publisher:19 Kirke Grove, Taunton, Somerset, TA2 8SB
I.S.B.N. 978-1-86241-049-7

© Trull Parish Archive Group, 2024
The authors assert their moral rights to be identified as the authors of this work. The publisher takes no repsonsibility for any opinions, content, images or indexing in this book.

CONTENTS

Preface to the second edition	iv
Preface to the first edition	vi
Acknowledgements	vii
Chapter 1 In the beginning	1
Chapter 2 Boundaries	4
Chapter 3 Population	7
Chapter 4 Early manorial history	10
Chapter 5 Early vernacular buildings by Mark McDermott	12
Chapter 6 Church history	29
Chapter 7 All Saints Church	37
Chapter 8 Church revenue and expenditure	48
Chapter 9 Life of Nicholas Heryng	55
Chapter 10 Women in the sixteenth century	57
Chapter 11 Civil strife	59
Chapter 12 The care of the poor	63
Chapter 13 Trull charities	67
Chapter 14 The farms of Trull updated by Graham Grant	72
Chapter 15 The School	95
Chapter 16 Queen's College	103
Chapter 17 Juliana Ewing	106
Chapter 18 Victorian memories	109
Chapter 19 Religious nonconformity by Mark McDermott	112
Chapter 20 Butcher, baker ...	115
Chapter 21 Halls and other amenities by Graham Grant	123
Chapter 22 The twentieth century and after	132
Glossary	146
Index	149

Preface to the second edition

In 1953, the Somerset Federation of Women's Institutes invited members to submit a history of their village as a County Coronation Year competition. Trull & Staplehay WI decided to enter, and Mrs Olive Hallam undertook the task of editor. In the event, no less than 116 entries were submitted – and Trull and Staplehay were awarded first prize. This consisted of a crystal goblet (see photo below) and framed certificate.

It was decided to publish *The Story of Trull*, and copies went on sale at 7s 6d (seven shillings and six pence) at Trull Post Office and the Dragon Bookshop in Taunton. Not surprisingly the first print of 200 copies sold out in three weeks, and it was hastily reprinted. Christmas cards were also published using some of the illustrations.

As you will see in the Preface to that first edition, the usual disclaimer was made about the lack of professional expertise in its compilation. This was somewhat disingenuous. Hidden amongst three pages of Acknowledgements is one to 'Mr AD Hallam for many suggestions and much information, criticism and encouragement'. He was Olive Hallam's husband – and a curator of the County Museum. Trull and Staplehay WI clearly had a head start!

~ The New History of Trull ~

Trull Parish Archive Group has been in existence since 2007, and is funded jointly by All Saints Church and Trull Parish Council. Publishing a new edition of *The Story of Trull* has been one of our ambitions since the beginning. Much new information has come to light in the past seventy-one years. For example, the WI's account starts in the Anglo-Saxon period, whereas a significant amount is now known about the prehistory of the area. Historical research, particularly by Mark McDermott and the late Cyril Green, has added substantially to our knowledge of the parish; as have reminiscences by long-term residents, such as the late Evelyn Solway's splendid book *A Trull Girl's Story,* published to mark her 90th birthday. But *The Story of Trull* remains an impressive and authoritative history, and the Parish Archive Group felt that we should bring this up-to-date in a new edition rather than attempt to write a new history of our parish. The first edition included two fold-out maps, one of Trull Parish as it was then, including the Tithings; and the other from the Tithe Apportionment Plan of 1842-3, including the field names. It has not proved feasible to reproduce these in this edition - the only map we have shown is in the chapter on Boundaries. Nor have we included the detailed references or acknowledgements from the first edition. But all of these can be consulted in copies of the original *The Story of Trull* held in the Trull Parish Archive.

Words not in common usage are explained in the Glossary at the end. We would be very glad to hear from you if you spot any errors in the book, if you feel that significant aspects of Trull's history have been overlooked, or if you have any items that you would like to donate to the parish archives. If so, please leave a note at the Church Office in the Trull Church Community Centre addressed to the Trull Parish Archive Group, and we will be in touch.

Preface to the first edition

In March 1953, when it was suggested at a meeting of Trull and Staplehay Women's Institute Committee that this book should be written, a member immediately objected: 'But Trull hasn't got any history'. If history means a record of stirring events and famous people, she was right. Even the Civil War and the Monmouth Rebellion do not seem to have affected the village very much; and the only notable man whom Collinson in his *History of Somersetshire* (1791) states to have been born in Trull was Sir George Bond, who became Lord Mayor of London and was a great-grandfather of the first Duke of Marlborough (and hence an ancestor of Sir Winston Churchill). But even this claim to fame is false, for Sir George Bond in his will proved in 1592 made a bequest to the 'Poor of Buckland where I was born', and his only apparent connection with Trull is that his sister married William Palmer of this parish. Collinson fills up the greater part of his page on Trull with an extract from the Bath Chronicle recording an interview in 1783 with Mrs Elizabeth Broadmead, who died a few months later aged 115.

No great family has ever lived in Trull, and there was never a resident lord of the manor to take a personal interest in the people. Prosperous yeomen and small gentry managed the affairs of the village for centuries. The story of Trull up to a hundred years ago is their story and that of small-holders and farm labourers, of the land they tilled and the church where they worshipped. The last hundred years have seen many changes; and today, though several of the farmers were born in the Parish, not one was born on the land he now farms; and, in an Institute with 75 members, only 5 were born in Trull.

No member of this Institute has had any previous experience of historical research, and for that reason it is hoped that the shortcomings of this book will be excused. The wealth of documents and printed sources available is so great that much has inevitably been neglected for lack of time.

Trull & Staplehay Women's Institute
1953

Acknowledgements

Trull Parish Archive Group is grateful to Trull & Staplehay Women's Institute, and particularly to its President, Shirley Welch, for permission to undertake a new edition of *The Story of Trull*, and for its encouragement in this project.

We have drawn heavily on the published works of Cyril Green, as acknowledged in the references at the end of each chapter. Cyril retired to Trull in 1976, having been Principal Lecturer in History and Deputy Principal of Goldsmiths' College, London University. He played a full part in the life of the parish, and gave the Parish Council Centenary Lecture in 1994. His talks, delivered fluently without notes, were legendary. He died in 1998.

We are also indebted to the late David Marks, born and bred in the parish. He played a leading part in the Scouts throughout his adult life, and was presented with the Somerset County Council Chairman's Award for Service to the Community. He shared his knowledge and enthusiasm for parish life in guided tours of the village, and in 'Just a thought …' a monthly column he wrote for many years in the Parish Magazine. These have been invaluable in our compiling a new edition of this parish history.

Ken Burge was very generous in his donations to the Parish Archive, which have been a great help to us. Ken was born and bred in Trull, and had a distinguished career in journalism. His first efforts were striking contributions to the Trull School Newsletter when he was a pupil there during the war, and he also edited *Camp Fire*, the local Scout newspaper. He then joined the Somerset County Gazette as a cub reporter, and rose through the ranks to eventually become the Editor in the 1980s. He played a very full part in parish life, and was Chairman of the Parish Council for some years. He kept all the files he accumulated in immaculate order, and it was these that he gave us along with many press cuttings and Minute Books of organisations he had been involved with, such as Trull Sports Club (see page 140).

Tom Mayberry's *The Vale of Taunton Past* has been a valuable resource. We are grateful to Robert Dunning, former Editor of the Victoria County History for Somerset, to Mary Siraut, the present Editor, and to Chris Webster, Manager of the Somerset Historic Environment Record at Somerset Heritage Centre, for their advice and support and to David Bromwich, Hon. Librarian of the Somerset Archaeological and Natural History Society and the Somerset Archives staff for their assistance in the Somerset Heritage Centre. And we would like to thank sincerely the many local people who have welcomed our visits to their properties, shared their knowledge with us, and encouraged us to take photographs to illustrate this book or provided them for us. The kind permission of Mr and Mrs S Eley, Shirley Hughes, and Martine Naughton to include photographs of the interiors of their houses in chapter 5 is also acknowledged, as is the assistance of Sarah Jeans with analysis of Middle Sweethay. Thanks must also go to the following for permitting photographs to be taken of their properties which feature in chapter 14, namely: Messrs W Derrick and M Lowe-Smith, Mr and Mrs W Venn, Mr and Mrs R Leamon, Colin Ralph, Susan Rose, Georgina Parris, Guy French, Mr and Mrs P Lord, Cmdr. J. Hurlbatt RN for the photograph of Reaphay Farm Cottages, Les Lock for the aerial photograph of Sweethay and Mr G Dusgate for permission to photograph Sweethay Court. In particular, we would like to thank Nick Chipchase for allowing us to reproduce photos and postcards from his extensive and impressive collection; the Somerset County Gazette for permission to reproduce photographs from their archive; and the South West Heritage Trust for allowing us to reproduce the photo by R Gillo as our Frontispiece (SHC, A/DIF/116/233).

Finally, our warm thanks to Debbie Crudge and Geoff Bisson for their assistance with the chapters on Trull School and Queen's College respectively, David Sharpe and Shirley Welch for their valuable comments on the draft, and to Adrian Webb for publishing this long-awaited volume.

This publication is supported by the Maltwood Fund of the Somerset Archaeological & Natural History Society.

1   In the beginning

Until quite recently, little was known about the prehistory of our area. But recent fieldwork has revealed important evidence of early human activity here. And archaeological surveys, in advance of motorway construction and planning applications, have also added to our knowledge.

Chris Norman in *The Archaeology of Somerset*[1] describes how highly mobile groups of early humans occupied the area intermittently during the Lower Palaeolithic period, from before 500,000 to about 250,000 years ago. We know this from the discovery of several hundred artefacts, all made of Greensand chert, including about a hundred complete and broken handaxes (see illustration) on Cotlake Hill, above Trull village, 'which suggests that this locality could have served as a temporary base for hominid groups who were engaged in procuring food from the adjacent valley'. He concludes that 'the quantity of artefacts present on the North side of Cotlake Hill places it amongst the more prolific findspots of surface palaeoliths in the country'.[2]

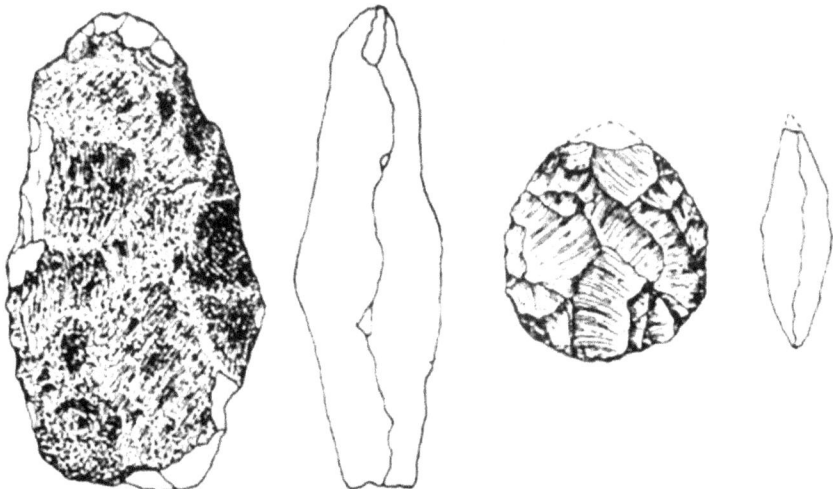

After that there is a long interval before any other evidence of human activity here, and it seems likely that climatic conditions made the area uninhabitable until about 60,000 years ago, and again from about 20,000 to 13,000 years ago.

The Somerset Historic Environment Record (HER)[3] includes a number of indications of features suggesting local prehistoric settlements, discovered by aerial photographs, excavations or recent geophysical surveys:

- at Cutsey, excavation work for the M5 motorway uncovered undated occupation evidence of a prehistoric settlement, and also Iron Age evidence north-east of Chilliswood Farm, 'cropmarks show clearly a large ... enclosure with a possible entrance'
- east of Higher Comeytrowe, an archaeological trench evaluation identified a wide combe feature containing Early to Middle Bronze Age (2,000 to 600 BC) pottery and an almost complete Early Bronze Age collared urn
- cropmarks seen in aerial photos of Castleman's Hill, in the north-west of the parish, were explored by an earthwork survey which revealed a double-ditched enclosure, of ovoid plan, probably a small promontory fort dating from the Iron Age (700 BC to AD 43)
- a geophysical survey and limited excavation at Broadlands, Staplehay, in support of a planning application[4] shows a circular enclosure, with postholes which appear to be part of a small timber structure, possibly late Neolithic or early Bronze Age, and provisionally identified as a henge.

Several individual prehistoric finds here are also included:

- worked chert, some with retouch, found on Cotlake Hill and identified as Mesolithic (9,500 to 5,500 years ago)
- a hammerstone, made from a quartzite pebble, in a garden on Amberd Lane, Trull: 'whilst it remains undated, a Palaeolithic to Neolithic origin is perhaps most likely'
- Neolithic flints, including one knife with a high dorsal ridge, location unrecorded other than 'Trull'.

There is some evidence of settlements during the Roman period, following the invasion of AD 43, east of Cutsey in the west of the parish, and at Poundisford Park, on the border with Pitminster parish. Roman pottery was unearthed at Higher Comeytrowe (see entry above); and Roman coins found in what is now Trull village, including a sestertius of Marcus Aurelius (AD 161-80) at Staplehay in 1866, and a 'second brass' of the early Roman empire whilst the Old Rectory in Wild Oak Lane was being built in 1908.

The area would have been cultivated by small farms throughout the Bronze Age and into the Roman period (and basically until today). There would have been a big change from the hunter/gatherer lifestyle of the early prehistoric period to farming, but this seems to have happened in the Bronze Age, not the Neolithic as was once thought.

The most recent archaeological survey in the parish was in support of the planning application[5] for an urban extension to Taunton on the fields between Trull and Comeytrowe, now known as Orchard Grove. It concluded that 'the assessment has demonstrated that there are no previously recorded sites, monuments or findspots located within the site, such that they should be considered within the development of an appropriate masterplan'. However, it also acknowledges that 'the site is within an area of high potential for the presence of Palaeolithic remains … there is, moreover, potential for the existence of Iron Age and Romano-British remains … it is likely that further archaeological investigation, in the form of geophysical survey and/or trial trenching, will be required to inform the determination of a planning application in the long term'. So who knows what further evidence of prehistoric life in our area may eventually turn up?

References
1. C Webster & T Mayberry, eds, *The Archaeology of Somerset*, Somerset County Council (2007), p.18.
2. C Norman, *Early Humans in the Vale of Taunton – a new perspective* in CJ Webster, ed, *Somerset Archaeology. Papers to mark 150 years of the Somerset Archaeological and Natural History Society*, Somerset County Council (2000).
3. The Somerset Historic Environment Record is managed for Somerset Council by the South West Heritage Trust, and can be found on the latter's website.
4. Taunton Deane BC planning application 42/15/0001, Archaeological Evaluation Report Parts 1-8.
5. Taunton Deane BC planning application 42/14/0069, Archaeological and Heritage Assessment.

2 Boundaries

The name Trull is probably derived from the Old English Trendel, meaning either a ring or circle,[1] though no evidence has yet been found of the former existence of any stone circle or earthwork which may have given rise to the name. The roughly circular shape of the churchyard before its enlargement may possibly be significant. The district known as Trendele or Trendle in medieval times was not the same as the area which formed Trull parish from the early 16th century until 1921.

The land now comprised in the present church and civil parishes of Trull (see map on page 6) formed part of a Saxon royal estate based on Taunton. Tradition records that a minster church was founded in the first half of the 8th century by Queen Frithogyth, who gave it to Winchester Cathedral.[2] The estate grew rapidly, including by a generous gift from King Aethelwulf in 854.

A charter reputed to date from that time gives the boundaries of this estate, although the landmarks are difficult to identify with present-day ones. The part of the boundary that passes though Trull village is described thus: 'So to the west through a certain grove to the stream called Scitere' (Sherford Stream). 'So by the course of the stream to the Old Ford'.[3] The probable position of the ford has been found by study in the field. Sherford Stream flows between high banks in the stretch from Staplehay Weir to Trull Meadow, but there was evidently a way down to it from the east on the south side of the Mill lane. The ford then seems to have followed the stream north for about 65 yards to leave it on the west bank at the only spot where there is a gradual slope. 'Hence to the West to the Deep Ford' (Dipford). So this part of the Saxon boundary seems to have continued for more than a thousand years as the traditional boundary between Trull and Pitminster parishes.

In 904 King Edward the Elder and Bishop Denewulf of Winchester agreed to exchange land they owned in Somerset and beyond. As a result, the Bishop and his successors became lords of the Manor of Taunton Deane, one of the largest and wealthiest in England. This included what is now the parish of Trull, hence the name of our village pub, the Winchester Arms. The Bishop's rights included:

- exemption of the minster at Taunton from all but the three common dues
- the bishop's men inhabiting there to be on the same legal footing as the king's men on royal estates
- the profits of justice, the burgage rents and market tolls of Taunton to be assigned to the bishop

- the abolition of duties which the men of Taunton had formerly performed for the king, including 'provision for one night's entertainment to the king, for 8 hounds and one dog-keeper, for the king's falconers for nine nights, cartage for any loads the king might wish to send, and escort for travellers from other regions to the next royal manor on their way'.[4]

In about 1120 the then Bishop of Winchester, William Giffard, founded Taunton Priory, reorganising the existing group of priests at the minster into a community of Augustinian canons, and this became the spiritual centre of the estate, from whence priests went to the villages to minister to the people there.[5] The administrative centre of the estate was Taunton Castle.

The countryside surrounding Taunton was known as the 'infaring' of the Manor of Taunton Deane, and was divided into five 'hundreds', including Hull and Poundisford in which the present parish of Trull was located. Beyond this was the 'outfaring' or 'liberty' of the estate, manors which acknowledged the bishop as overlord and owed attendance at his courts in Taunton, but otherwise functioned independently.[6] By 1327 the infaring hundreds had been sub-divided into tithings. Those which came within the present parish of Trull were Wodelonde (Woodland), in the south-west of the parish; Dupeforde (Dipford); and Northtrendle (Southtrendle was in the parish of Pitminster). These tithings continued to be the administrative units of the manor and parish until 1834. From that date the parish in its ecclesiastical form was the unit of civil administration until the north-eastern corner was transferred to the borough of Taunton in 1921.

'Parish' can now mean one of two things. The civil parish is the first tier of local government, and since 1894 a Parish Council has been elected every four years by all the residents in the parish. No woman had ever been a member of Trull Parish Council until, in 1952, the first election by secret ballot took place, when two women were elected. Its meetings are open to all. Not all places are parished in this way, particularly in urban areas. And secondly there is the ecclesiastical parish, the catchment area of the local Church of England parish church. Members on its electoral roll annually elect a Parochial Church Council, which meets in closed sessions. The boundaries of these two parishes are often not coterminous, as is the case in Trull.

Our parish boundaries were eventually changed to reflect post-war development. In 1969 Staplehay, Eastbrook, Kibbear and Brown's Elm at last became part of All Saints Parish rather than of Pitminster church. At the same time, the housing developments to the north of the church parish – Somerset Avenue, Deane Drive and Claremont – were transferred to St George's Wilton, to be followed in 1993 by the new estate of New Barn Park, east of Comeytrowe Road.

In 1983 the civil parish of Comeytrowe was created from the north-east part of Trull parish and part of the Borough of Taunton, and Trull parish boundary to the south and east took in what had been the northern part of Pitminster parish, as far as the line of the new M5 motorway, opened in 1974, including the development at Killams. Forty years later, in 2023, Comeytrowe Parish was absorbed into the new Taunton Parish, as were the Trull parish areas covered by the Orchard Grove development and Killams Green. However, Orchard Grove remains in the ecclesiastical parish of Trull.

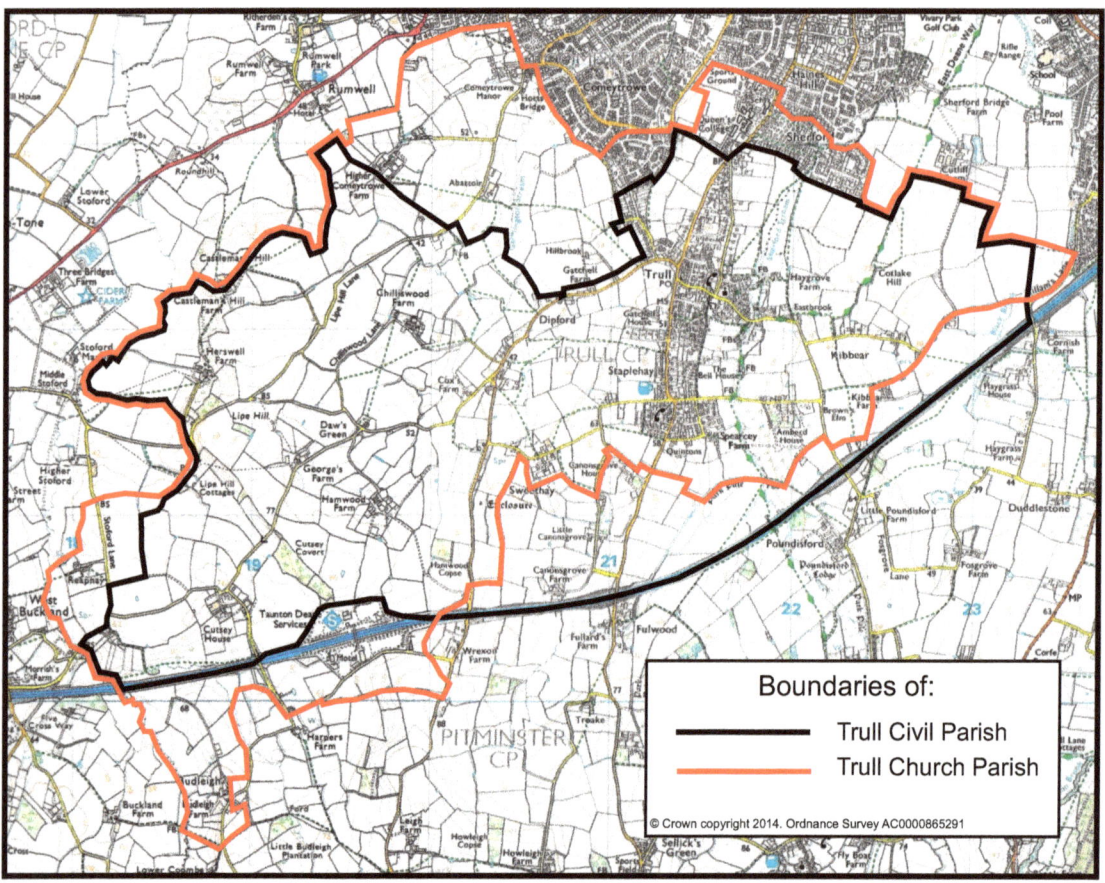

References
1. E Ekwall, *Oxford Dictionary of English Place-Names* (1960).
2. RJE Bush, *The Book of Taunton*, Barracuda Books (1977), p.22.
3. GB Grundy, *The Saxon Charters of Somerset* (1935).
4. HPR Finberg, *The Early Charters of Wessex*, Leicester University Press (1964).
5. S Membury, *Taunton Priory Excavation*, Somerset County Council (2013), p.6.
6. T Mayberry, *The Vale of Taunton Past*, Phillimore & Co (1998).

3 Population

The people of Trull must have been almost all engaged in agriculture until the 19th century. From the Certificate of Musters in 1569 it appears that nobody in any of the three Tithings of Trull (South Trendle was then in Pitminster parish) held land worth more than £10 a year, because neither horses nor firearms were listed among the warlike equipment provided.

More variation in wealth is apparent from the Hearth Tax return made about a hundred years later. John Baker was the only man ranked as 'gent' and he owned 13 hearths including those in cottages belonging to him. John Thomas had two hearths but he stopped up one, obviously to save paying the 2s tax on it. Two cottages each worth less than a pound a year were exempt from tax, and two more were in the possession of very poor tenants 'not rated to church nor poore'. William Buncombe made out that he had one hearth when he really owned three, and two others also made false returns.

The rent roll of the Bishop of Winchester for 1744-5 shows that the 'Lord's Rent' payable by inhabitants of Trull parish varied from £5 12s 9d to 4d.

The following table gives tentative estimates of the population of the then parish of Trull from the 16th to the 18th century, based on the sources mentioned above and the church seating plans.

YEAR	1569	1635	1647	1664-5	1744-5
Approx. no. of adults	166	187			
No. of hearths				124	
No. of holdings of land			82		
Estimated no. of inhabitants	332	374	369	372	396

From 1801 onwards the census returns (on page 8) give accurate information. The graph below shows the populations of the then parish of Trull and the adjoining parish of Pitminster, which covered a far larger area and was more purely rural than Trull. Eastbrook, Kibbear, Staplehay, Sweethay and Canonsgrove were all in Pitminster parish until 1983.

The Pitminster figures show an almost unbroken rise from 1801 to 1871, after which time the drift from the land is reflected by a steady fall until 1931. Robert Dunning describes the rural poverty identified by Acland and Sturge in their study *Agriculture in Somerset* in 1851: 'The problem was really one of over population, and its solution emigration. From the high water mark of 1841 the rural population of the county fell dramatically, in some villagers by nearly a half in a few years'.[1]

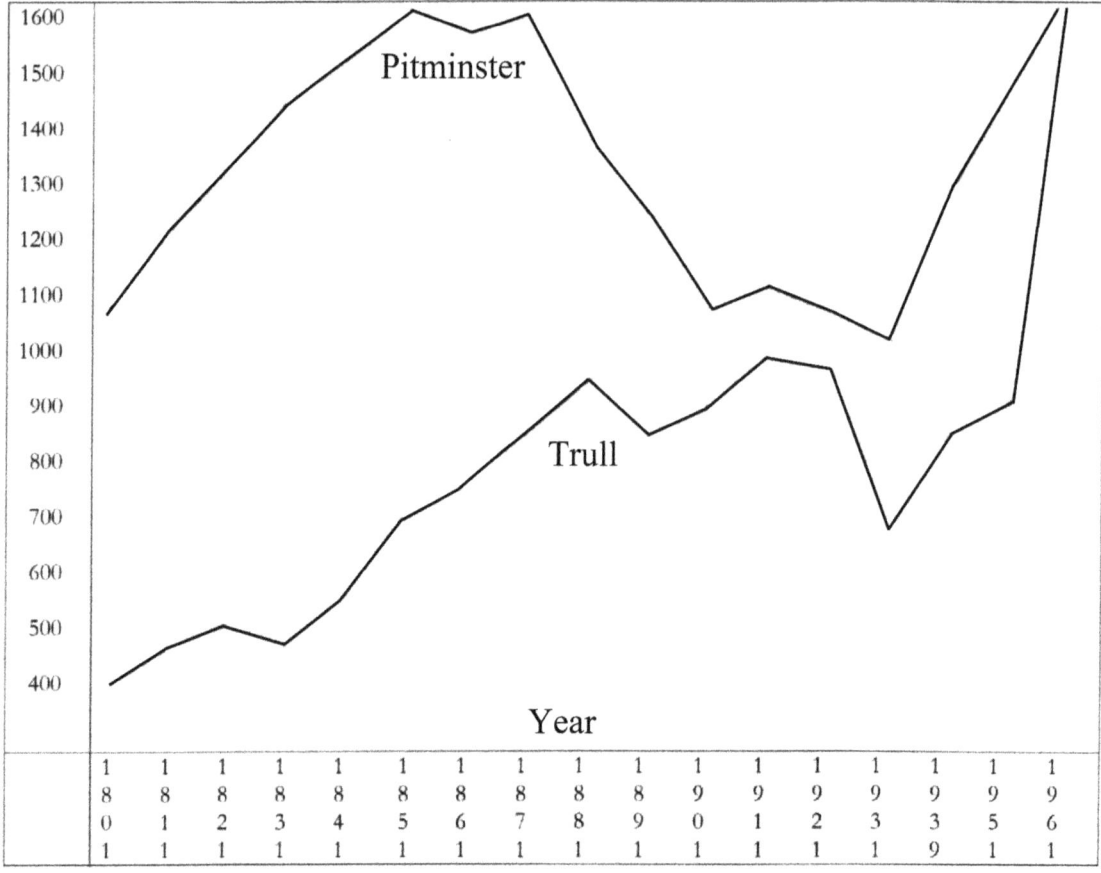

POPULATION GRAPH

The figures for 1939 are those of the National Registration enumeration on the outbreak of WW2, and the rise in that year in both parishes was doubtless due to evacuation. The beginning of several trends which continued are implicit in the following table for Trull:

YEAR	1811	1831
Families engaged in Agriculture	83	67
Families engaged in Trade, Manufacture or Handicrafts	12	18
All other families	3	16
No. of Males	251	250
No. of Females	248	256

The graph for Trull rises steadily from 1831 to 1861, during which time the population of the whole country was increasing rapidly. Prosperous businessmen and farmers retired and built substantial houses such as Gatchell House, Hillbrook House, Dipford House, Wild Oak,

The Lawn and White Lodge, some of which incorporated much older buildings. The agricultural depression probably accounts for the fall between 1881 and 1891, but the population of Trull rose again whilst that of Pitminster was still falling; this must have been due to the increasing popularity of the Haines Hill district as a residential suburb of Taunton. This part of the parish was transferred to the borough in November 1921, which accounts for the sharp fall between 1921 and 1931. Loss of life and drift to the towns in the 1914-18 war may be the cause of the slight fall between 1911 and 1921.

There has been a steady rise following WW2, with relatively small-scale developments in Trull and Staplehay, such as Wyatt's Field, Brookside Close, Trull Green Drive, Park Close, Sweethay Close, Furlong Green, Dipford Orchard, Gatchell Oaks and Amingford Grange. Some of these have been on the site of demolished Victorian villas, such as Claremont (now Coplestons) and Southhay (now Southwell).

At the 2001 Census the population of the current civil parish (see map on page 6) was 2,288, with slightly more females than males (they live longer on average). 55 (2.4%) had described themselves as 'Black and Minority Ethnic', compared with 14% for England & Wales as a whole. 27% were 65 or older, compared with 21% for Somerset as a whole and 17% for England & Wales. A total of 13 persons were engaged in agriculture and 65 in manufacturing, which makes an interesting contrast with the figures in the table above.

Reference
RW Dunning, *A History of Somerset* (2003), p.89.

4 Early manorial history

There is no mention of Trull or Trendle in the Domesday Book of 1086, unlike neighbouring Pitminster, for example. This is because Trull, Wilton, Staplegrove and Bishops Hull were all included in the Taunton entry, as part of the Bishop of Winchester's huge estate. 'There the bishop has 80 villeins (villagers), 82 bordars (smallholders), 70 slaves, 16 coliberts (freedmen), 17 swineherds, who pay £7 10s,[1] 64 burgesses (townsmen) who render 32s; there the bishop has 8 riding horses, 30 cattle (including plough oxen), 24 pigs, 100 sheep; 3 mills which pay £4 15s, woodland a league long and a league wide, 40 acres of meadow, pasture 2 leagues long and 1 league wide; a market rendering 50s'.[2]

The men and stock of the Bishop of Winchester in Taunton from the Exeter Domesday. Photograph by Exeter University Photographic Unit.

The pipe roll of the Bishopric of Winchester for the year 1207-8 gives detailed accounts of the revenue and expenditure of the Manor of Taunton Deane. The statement of accounts for the Infaring Manor, which included 'Trindele', was rendered by Willelmus de Sorewella in Latin. The tenants of the manor held their land from the bishop, to whom they paid Lord's Rent, and though they could sell their holding and could leave it to their heirs, a fine (fee) had to be paid to the lord of the manor on every change of tenancy. As well as Lord's Rent the peasants had to give their labour, but payment was made for work done on Saturdays. In Trindele 4s 6d was paid for 36 Saturdays. Two ploughmen and one foreman received 3s 9d, and seven labourers 1s 9d, as a rebate of rent in return for work done over and above their customary service.

The same year 66 acres of land were sown with 15½ quarters of seed wheat, and 81 acres with 54 quarters of seed oats. No barley or rye was sown. Trindele was the only tithing in the district where a crop of peas was grown. Two quarters of seed were bought specially, and eight acres sown. Seven quarters of food was used for two cattle sheds. At haymaking and harvest three quarters two 'hopae' (heaped bushels) of wheat were given to the labourers, and 6d was spent on buying a relish for them to spread on their bread at the Harvest Home.

Miscellaneous expenses at Trendle were as follows:

> For shoeing of plough horses 6d.
> For the smith's wages 2s.
> For special work in winter and at Quadragesima of 29 ploughmen 2s 5d.
> For food for the foreman and two ploughmen as perquisites at Christmas and Easter 6d.
> For food for seven labourers and two maidservants by way of the same perquisite 8d.
> For repairs to ploughs, for putting axles to carts and for repairs, with purchase of grease and yokes 1s 4½d.
> For one pair of wheels for a cart 3s.
> For carrying forage from Pundl(esforda) (?Poundisford) to the barton 3d.

At the courts held at Taunton Castle money was exacted for various offences, and the accounts show that Philip of Cochage paid 2s for a breach of the peace, Robert of Depeforda (Dipford) 12s for contempt of court, and a whole tithing had to pay 2s for concealment of an offence.

The mills of Pitminster and Trindele were farmed out to William of Swafam for £5. He was evidently not the miller, but one of the salaried officials of the Bishopric. His salary for 282 days amounted to about £2 7s and he was allowed 4s for fur to embellish his clothes.

References
1. Before decimal coinage replaced it in 1971, the pound sterling (£) had sub-units of 20 shillings (s. from Latin *solidi*) to a pound, 12 pence (d. from Latin *denarii*) to a shilling, 2 ha'pence (½d.) and, until 1960, 4 farthings (¼d.) to a penny.
2. RW Dunning, *Somerset in Domesday*, Somerset County Council Library Service (1986), p.11.

5   Early vernacular buildings in Trull

The houses of the parish include a number of early vernacular buildings dating from the medieval period and the 16C and 17C and constructed of traditional local materials: cob, stone, occasional timber-framing and one instance of 17C brick (Hamwood) for walls and, originally, thatch for roofs. Most seem to have had a traditional farmhouse plan of three rooms in line, with a 'hall' (a room, not an entrance hall) in the centre, an 'inner' room or parlour at one end, and, on the other side of the hall, a cross-passage and an 'outer' or service room, although in the case of a 'longhouse' this end of the house would accommodate livestock in a byre.

In the medieval period the hall, and possibly the whole house, would have been open to the roof, but during the 16C there was a growing fashion for houses to be built or updated with an upper floor. The hall now had to have an enclosed fireplace and in Somerset this was usually positioned so that it backed onto the cross-passage, although in some cases it took the form of a 'lateral' stack on the front or back wall of the hall: front stacks are a special characteristic of vernacular architecture in the area between Dunster and Porlock (and in Devon) but there is an outstanding example in Gatchell Cottage in Trull. Houses with the 3-room plan were commonly enlarged with wings, lean-tos and other extensions during the 16C and onwards.

Several early houses in Trull parish have roofs of post-and-truss and jointed-cruck design. Jointed crucks, which are a particular characteristic of many vernacular buildings in Somerset and Devon, have crucks (curving blades) each made of a pair of timbers scarf-jointed together, perhaps because of a shortage of suitable timber for full-length blades in the 15C/16C. The drawing below shows a jointed–cruck truss at Chilliswood (see page 76) (by permission of Somerset Vernacular Building Research Group).

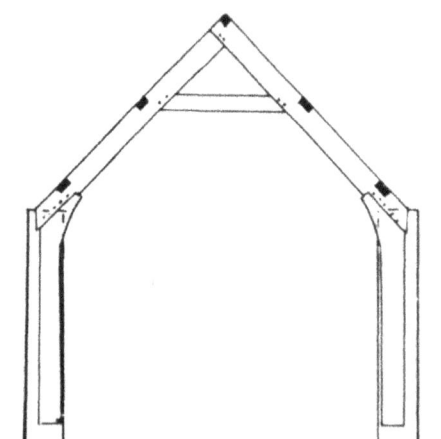

The scattered locations of these houses within the parish are evidence of a dispersed settlement pattern from an early date (possibly from the beginning of settlement in this area) and the tithe map of 1842 and the 6 inch Ordnance Survey map of 1888 show that the present 'nucleated' pattern in the general vicinity of the church has largely come about since the 19C.

King's Gatchell

This much altered and extended house, as illustrated with the west wing on the right, includes a long N-S range which may originally have had a 3-room and cross-passage plan. Desmond Williams, in 1988, thought that the outer room (on the N), which has thinner walls (including brick) and a slight change of alignment, might be a later addition to an original 2-room plan in which there would have been a cross-passage between the hall and the room to the S. The original walls of the house are reputed to be of cob but, if so, this is hidden by rendering. The roof of the N-S range has been heightened and various additions, including a W wing and entrance turret, have been made in the 18C, 19C and 1920s. There is also a lodge (now in private hands), coach-house and stables (converted to other uses) but a suggestion that the house was once a coaching inn has not been confirmed.

The hall has a 9-panel framed ceiling and a large fireplace, with moulded jambs and lintel, which may have replaced a smoke-bay (an early type of fireplace). Above the room to the S of the hall is a first-floor chamber which has a plastered cruck truss (jointed?) and fine early-17C decorative plasterwork including Tudor rose, fleur-de-lys and, under a floral arcade, royal arms (lion and unicorn) and initials I R for Iacobus Rex (James I, 1603-1625).

John and Jane Penoyre have found parallels between this plasterwork and that in the Hankridge Arms in Taunton and Ashe Farm, Thornfalcon. The arms must be a display of loyalty by a former owner, as there is no evidence that James I had any connection with the house.

In the early 19C the property was known as Lower Gatchell, later as Southwick House, but by 1889 it had become King's Gatchell. Gatchell has been recorded as a surname in the parish

since at least the 16C. 19C owners of the property included Dr Harness, a retired physician, Col. England and Major General Emerson. Miss Wigram, a devout Catholic, who lived here from 1902-36, was a benefactor to the village who gave the site for the first Village Hall, built in 1921. In her will she intended the house to become a religious house, but Buckfast Abbey and two London convents did not take advantage of the offer.

On page 14 is Miss Wigram's drawing in c.1902 of the view from a bedroom window of the house down Church Road. Vine Cottage, on the right at the end of the High Path, was then part of the property. On the left is Mr Whale's orchard, hence the name Orchard Close when housing was built there in the 1950s and '60s. The other cottages are still there, those in the middle being Lilac Cottages.

References
SHC, DD/V/TAR/29/1 EHD Williams, vernacular architecture report in 1988.
J & J Penoyre, *Decorative Plasterwork in the Houses of Somerset 1500-1700*, Somerset County Council (1994).
CW Green, *Trull and Staplehay with an eye on the past* (1993). Additional information from Andy Adam, who lived in the house from 1994 to 2006.

Haygrove
This former farmhouse (to a farm previously known as Batts) when surveyed in 1992 consisted of a complex of buildings around a small central courtyard, which included residential accommodation and ancillary structures.

The earliest part of the complex is the south range (aligned E-W), which is believed to be built of cob on a stone base and on the ground floor consists of two rooms separated by a cross-passage. To the west of the cross-passage is a room, originally the service room, with a deep fireplace suitable for cooking, and to the east is the hall with a fireplace backing onto the cross-passage. The original house may have had an inner room to the east of the hall, demolished when the east range of the house was built.

The south range has a king-post roof (probably 19C) but the upright posts of several jointed crucks survive from an earlier roof which could be medieval or 16/17C in origin. The range has two storeys but may originally have had an open hall.

The east range (aligned N-S and on the left of the photograph) is believed to be built of stone under rendering and is taller than the south range. It has a hipped roof with oversailing eaves, and sash windows. It is believed to date from c.1800 and formerly had a veranda along the east front. Other parts of the complex seem to have been added later.

Immediately to the north of the farmhouse is a detached water mill, originally fed by a leat which flowed from a sluice gate off the Sherford Stream at Staplehay Weir to the Mill Pond beside Haygrove Farmhouse and thence past the west side of the house. The mill has been converted into a dwelling, but some of the machinery survives and remains of the water wheel are still visible today (2023). To the east of the mill is a farm outbuilding originally built of cob on a stone base but the walls are now encased or partially rebuilt in brick. The roof has jointed crucks similar to those formerly in the south range of the house.

The farm consisted of 62 acres in 1838, but 160 acres in 1901 when it was part of the estate of the late Revd Beauchamp Kerr-Pearse which was being auctioned. The estate included Batts Park, and the farm, which included Hillside Farm, Hillside Cottage and Trull Meadow, was referred to as 'Haygrove and Batts Farm' (Haygrove House being the 'respectable and commodious Farm Residence'). The farm was again for sale in 1963 but since 1989 Haygrove has been a private house, now divided in two.

References
CW Green, *Trull and Staplehay with an eye on the past*, Trull School (1993).
Trull Parish Archive, MB McDermott, Vernacular architecture report, 1992.
Trull Parish Archive, Auction particulars in 1901 and 1963.

Chantry Cottage
This cottage, next to the north-west corner of the churchyard in Wild Oak Lane, was formerly known as Clerk's Cottage (as in 1843, when its owners were recorded as the parish officers). It was lived in by successive parish clerks until Samuel Doble became the last parish clerk to live there. In the 1530s work was done on the house of the parish clerk John Haynysworthe,

which may be an early reference to this building.

The cottage, aligned N-S, has a 2-room plan with a later lean-to extension at the N end. The walls of the original 2-room part are of cob on a low stone base, with a later brick skin on the W side and N gable, but the S end, which incorporates a winding stair and a fireplace and stack, is built of a mixture of dressed Hamstone, lias blocks and pieces of chert and brick. The roof is thatched.

There is an entrance to the cottage in the E wall, but there is no clear evidence that there was formerly a cross-passage. A stud-and-plank partition separates the two rooms, the N of which may originally have been an unheated parlour. It has a moulded framed ceiling, but the beams have been reused from elsewhere and cut to fit the space.

The S room has deeply chamfered transverse beams (two with zig-zag painted decoration) with deep step-stops at the ends of the chamfers. Two of the beams are aligned with the posts of two jointed-cruck trusses, but another corresponds with the posts of a post-and-truss structure above the partition. One of the truss posts includes redundant joints (seen by Williams in 1975) implying former timber-framed walls, here or elsewhere (if this is a reused timber).

Internally, the stone S end wall contains a fireplace with a shallow four-centred arched lintel (16C?) and double-ogee mouldings, also the remains of a bread-oven. On the upper floor, which rises into the roof and is lit by dormer or gable windows, the two rooms are separated by a post-and-truss structure (with tie-beam and collar), and there is a similar truss in the N gable-end wall, both with wattle-and-daub infilling. In the S room the upper parts of the two jointed-cruck trusses are also visible. The marked contrast between the roofs in the N and S parts of the cottage, together with (a) a difference in the ceiling heights of the two rooms on the ground floor, (b) evidence of a former stairway through the ceiling of the N room and (c) the fact that access between the two first-floor rooms has been made by cutting through a tie-beam, suggests that the S half of the building was originally an open hall. If so, the winding stair must be a later insertion, and perhaps the entire S end stone wall was an addition to the original building.

References
SHC, DD/V/TAR/29/9 & 29/14 Cdr Williams, vernacular architecture reports, 1975 and 1990.
EHD Williams, 'The Building Materials of Somerset's Vernacular Houses' in *Somerset Archaeology and Natural History*, vol. 135 (1991), pp.123-134.
CW Green, *Trull and Staplehay with an eye on the past*, Trull School (1993).
RW Dunning and MB McDermott, eds, *Church Accounts 1457-1559*, Somerset Record Society vol. 95 (2013), pp. 235-303.

Vine Cottage

This cottage, with rendered walls and a tiled roof, was originally a 3-room and cross-passage house (aligned E-W) of which the service room and cross-passage at the E end have been demolished and replaced with a modern rebuild. The remaining part of the original house consists of the hall which has a framed ceiling and a large fireplace backing onto the cross-passage, and, to the west, an inner room, originally unheated, from which a passage has been partitioned off to provide access to a stairway. The position of the beams of the framed ceiling indicates that the front and back walls of the house were originally much thicker internally and have been rebuilt (perhaps stone replacing cob).

The three roof trusses over the earlier part of the house have smoke-blackening over the hall but not over the inner room. The hall was therefore open to the roof (in the 15C) and heated by an open hearth, and the fireplace, chimney stack and framed ceiling are insertions of the 16/17C.

Vine Cottage at one time belonged to King's Gatchell and was linked to it by the high wall next to the footpath which was raised to avoid floodwater.

References
SHC, DD/V/TAR/29/13 Cdr Williams, vernacular architecture report in 1988.
CW Green, *Trull and Staplehay with an eye on the past*, Trull School (1993).

Dipford Farm

This house, which has evidence of cob beneath the rendered walls, has remnants of a jointed-cruck roof and is another cross-passage house. When examined internally in 1982, the room on the N side of the cross passage included a large blocked fireplace and would have functioned as the service room. The hall on the S side of the passage had a substantial fireplace backing onto the passage and a 6-panel framed ceiling with hollow-chamfered beams. To the S of the hall are, unusually, two further rooms, that at the S end of the house having another 6-panel framed ceiling. The plan, the ceilings and some other features suggest a date no later than the 16C or early 17C for the main range of the house. The house was recorded in 1664 (for hearth tax purposes) as having four hearths.

Changes in floor level on the first floor suggest that the house originally had a medieval open hall (15C?), which was subsequently floored over. The replacement of the upper parts of the jointed-cruck roof, with a later roof, has deprived the house of potential evidence of smoke-blackening to confirm the 'open hall' theory.

The house has wings at the SW and NE corners, a lean-to on the W, and a NE attached outbuilding with a plaque dated 1808. That building and the lean-to are clearly additions, as may be the wings, albeit at an earlier date (17C?).

The earliest identified holder of the farm (within the Manor of Taunton Deane) is Thomas Keene who died in 1540 and was succeeded by his son Thomas in 1541. The property continued in the family until 1688 when it was inherited by Elizabeth Keene who had married John Cranmer of West Buckland. When this or another John Cranmer died in 1731 he left it to his nephew and heir John Jenkins from whom it was acquired by Jane Strickland, a widow, in 1751. It was inherited by her son Joseph and then by his brother Edward who had let it to Robert Mattock by 1807. The plaque recording an extension to the house in 1808 includes the initials RM.

In 1826 Edward Strickland died, leaving the farm to Mattock, on whose death in 1835 it was inherited by his eight children, but George Matthews, husband of Mattock's daughter Susannah, purchased the shares of the other seven heirs to become owner. Cyril Green has listed a succession of owners from then until 1963 when it was bought by Dr and Mrs Parry Jones, and it has remained in the family since then.

References
Historical information in a letter from Ivor Collis, County Archivist, to Dr Parry Jones, 16 July 1964 (copy held by MB McDermott) and in a letter from Dr Parry Jones to MB McDermott, 17 Sept. 1982.
CW Green, *Trull and Staplehay with an eye on the past*, Trull School (1993).
SHC, DD/V/TAR/29/10 MB McDermott, vernacular architecture report, 1982.

Gatchell Cottage and Gatchell Spinney
These two cottages in Dipford Road occupy what was formerly a medieval house which had an open hall (partly floored over with a loft), a screens passage (now a cross passage), a service room (believed to have been open to the roof) to the W of the passage, and an inner room (now part of Gatchell Spinney) to the E of the hall. The rendered walls contain cob, but

there is evidence of original timber-framing. There is a timber-framed jetty on the front which is believed to have been added in the 16C when the service room was divided and floored over. Gatchell Spinney has an inserted front door which replicates the early front door into the cross passage, and the building has been extended to the E.

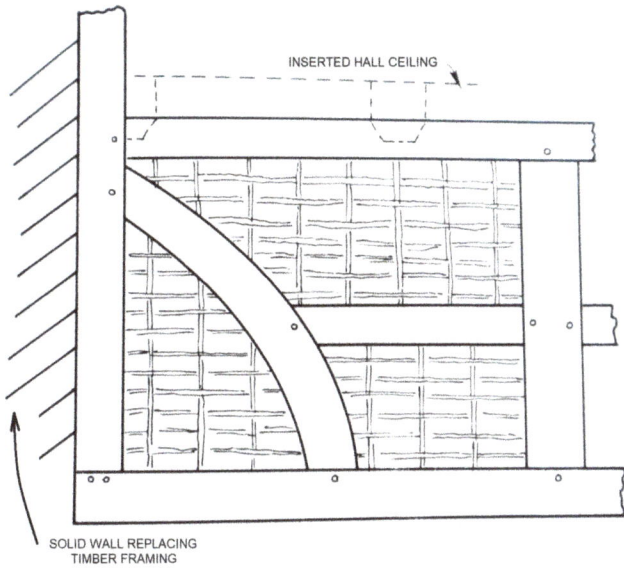

The chimney stack projecting from the front of the hall is thought to be a 17C replacement for an earlier fireplace. Various interesting internal features include the roof, which includes, over the formerly open hall, a post-and-truss structure at each end and a central arch-braced jointed-cruck truss. The drawing by Williams is of an internal partition with curved brace and wattle-and-daub panels (by permission of Somerset Archaeological & Natural History Society).

These two photographs show part of an open arch-braced jointed–cruck truss (now infilled) over the hall, and a post-and-truss frame above the jetty.

At one time the cottages belonged to Gatchell House and were lived in by employees there.

References
SHC, DD/V/TAR/29/7 Cdr Williams, vernacular architecture reports, 1975 and 1977.
Cdr Williams, 'The Building Materials of Somerset's Vernacular Houses' in *Somerset Archaeology and Natural History*, Vol. 135 (1991), pp. 123-134.
CW Green, *Trull and Staplehay with an eye on the past*, Trull School (1993).

Boxenhedge
This two-storey house, with its wide asymmetrical N front and Doric porch, has rendered walls under a slated (but formerly thatched) roof. Some cob walls may be survivors from an earlier house, but the plan was altered and the house updated, including sash windows and various internal features, in the first half of the 19C, and there have been other changes since then.

The property was owned by the Buncombe family for over two hundred years until widow Elizabeth Buncombe sold the house and 34 acres of land in 1798 to silversmith Robert Foy who leased it, together with some land, to Reuben Bicknell. By 1841 the occupants were Susannah Bicknell, 65; another Susannah Bicknell, 20, and her sister, 15, both described as schoolmistresses; and a dozen young 'pupils'. The house was evidently now used as a boarding school. In 1842 it was leased, with its land, from a new owner, Dr Daniel Pring; and by 1851 the property was occupied by auctioneer Richard Greenslade, his family and two servants. James White, farmer and churchwarden, lived there in the 1870s and 1880s, and some 20C occupants have been identified by Cyril Green.

References
SHC, DD/V/TAR/29/16 Somerset Vernacular Building Research Group report, 2018.
CW Green, *Trull and Staplehay with an eye on the past*, Trull School (1993).

Kibbear Farm
This farmhouse incorporates an early-17C building, with cob walls and the familiar vernacular 3-room and cross-passage plan. The hall fireplace backs onto the cross-passage in the usual way and there are chamfered and stopped beams and a roof which includes jointed crucks and post-and-truss structures, although there is no evidence of a former open hall. To this early building have been added various later additions on the E front and elsewhere, including domestic facilities and outbuildings (when surveyed in 1988).

According to Cyril Green the acreage of the farm grew from 56 to 180 acres between 1838 and 1881, and it was farmed by the Spiller family from the 1870s until the 1940s, after which it was farmed by Harold Small for the next 40 years. A photograph of the farmhouse can be found on page 85.

References
SHC, DD/V/TAR/21/27 Cdr Williams, vernacular architecture report, 1988.
CW Green, *Trull and Staplehay with an eye on the past*, Trull School (1993).

Kibbear Cottages

These two semi-detached cottages originated as a 3-room and cross-passage house, of which the hall and inner room now form part of a distinct dwelling which has been heightened and modernised, but the remainder (the area of the cross-passage and outer room) has retained its low eaves and thatched roof and is entered by a doorway with a heavy chamfered frame and curved head. The walls are rendered (cob?). A small wing added later at the front of this second cottage includes a small 4-light wooden window with trefoil heads to the lights, an early but reused feature.

Internally, when examined in 1988, the area of the cross-passage and outer room had been reorganized into two rooms and a large fireplace at the gable wall had been blocked by a stove. A winding stair next to the fireplace provided access to the upper floor. The roof included a cruck truss (probably jointed, but the joint was not visible) and a post-and-truss structure. It is thought that the house dates from at least the early 16C and was originally open to the roof, and the long outer room could have been a byre for livestock (at the downhill end of the sloping site), implying that this could have been a longhouse.

Reference
SHC, DD/TAR/V/21/28 Cdr Williams, vernacular architecture report, 1988.

Amberd Farmhouse

This former farmhouse, aligned E-W on sloping ground, is built mainly of cob (plastered and whitewashed) with a thatched roof. Smoke-blackening inside the roof (which may have jointed crucks, although the joints were not visible when the house was examined in 1985) indicates that at least the W half of the house was once open to the roof and therefore medieval in origin. Scroll-stopped beams indicate that the upper floor was inserted in the early 17C, which is presumably when the projection containing a stairway at the rear of the house was built.

The plan includes a cross-passage with a service room to the W (including a deep fireplace with a bread oven inserted into a former curing chamber on one side of the fireplace) but to the E the plan is unusual, with three rooms instead of the usual two, and a second front door has been inserted. The first of the three rooms seems to be too small for a medieval hall, and the room at the E end of the house may be an addition. It is thought that the hall may originally have included the area of the cross-passage and service room and that the building may have been a longhouse which extended further W down the slope.

The farm belonged to Amberd House in the 19C and subsequently to Eastbrook House, Mark Sparks being the tenant farmer between 1910 and 1939. The farmhouse was separated from its land when the Eastbrook estate was sold in 1961 and subsequent owners of the house have included Major and Mrs Nicholl.

References
SHC, DD/V/TAR/21/25 RG Gilson, vernacular architecture report, 1985.
CW Green, *Trull and Staplehay with an eye on the past*, Trull School (1993).

Canonsgrove Farmhouse
As described by Williams in 1976, this farmhouse, thought to date from the 16C, has a range of interesting internal and external features, including some 17C windows. The plan includes a hall with a fireplace backing onto a cross-passage, beyond which is an outer room with a projecting bread-oven behind a deep fireplace, and to one side of the outer room is a wing. Beyond the hall is an inner room containing an inserted stairway, and beyond that another room has been added to the plan. Exposed quoin stones in an external wall may suggest that the house originally had a two-room plan which was extended by the addition of the cross-passage and outer room in the 17C, and the wing possibly at the same time.

The partition between the hall and inner room is set within a cruck truss but any joints are concealed by plaster. The hall itself has decorative wall panelling (including fluted pilasters) which may have been reused; and a first-floor room above the outer room has a decorative plaster ceiling in 17C style, with panels, a cornice and frieze and various motifs including roses, grapes, foliage, animals, birds and angel heads with wings. This ceiling is an unusually ornate feature for a farmhouse of that period. A photograph of the farmhouse can be found in Chapter 14.

Reference
SHC, DD/V/TAR/21/8 Cdr Williams, vernacular architecture report, 1976.

Little Canonsgrove
Externally the walls of this former farmhouse have a mixture of white-washed rendering and exposed chert and lias stone, and the roof is slated but was probably originally thatched. The only early window is a mullioned stone window, with 17C ovolo mouldings, in the E gable wall as shown in the photograph which also shows a lean-to at the rear of the house. This is another house which, according to a survey by Ron Gilson in 1984, includes a cross-passage and 3-room plan, to which was added a fourth room beyond the outer or service room, and a lean-to at the rear.

The hall has a six-panel framed ceiling which may have been inserted into an open hall, and

a fireplace in the service room has replaced a smoke-bay (an early form of fireplace). The roof has a mixture of post-and-truss frames and jointed crucks. The house is thought to date from the 16C, with the added room and hall ceiling being inserted in the later 16C and a fireplace replacing the smoke-bay in the 17C.

Reference
SHC, DD/V/TAR/21/23 RG Gilson, vernacular architecture report, 1984.

Sweethay
This hamlet, which straddles the former parish boundary between Trull and Pitminster, includes **Sweethay Court,** formerly a 3-room and cross-passage farmhouse known as Higher Sweethay Farm until much altered and renamed when it became a private residence in the 20C. **Middle Sweethay**, as illustrated below, has rendered walls, low eaves, dormer windows (renewed) and evidence of a previously thatched roof and retains much of its early character. It is a 3-room and cross-passage house in which the outer room (still without a fireplace) may formerly have stored food and drink, or even accommodated livestock. Over the hall, smoke-blackened roof timbers, including crucks (not jointed), arch-braces and a surviving wind-brace indicate that the house has medieval (14C?) origins. The hall has a framed ceiling inserted in the 16C or early 17C, and a rear wing was added to the house, perhaps as a kitchen, in the 17C.

Lower Sweethay was recorded by Williams in 1988 as a two-storey house built of rubble stone (roughcast) under a tiled roof, with a 3-room and cross-passage plan, later extended by an additional room beyond the inner room, and the front entrance to the cross-passage has been blocked. Internally, Williams recorded a 9-panel framed ceiling in the hall, and smoke-blackened roof trusses indicating that the hall (including a central arch-braced truss as a visual feature) was once open to the roof. The ceiling and hall fireplace (which backs onto the cross-passage in typical fashion and may have replaced a smoke louvre, for which Williams found some limited evidence) are therefore later insertions into a medieval open-hall house. The photograph shows the fireplace and framed ceiling in the hall.

References
SHC, DD/V/TAR/29/12 Cdr Williams, vernacular architecture report on Lower Sweethay Farm, 1988.

CW Green, *Trull and Staplehay with an eye on the past*, Trull School (1993). Middle Sweethay: vernacular architecture report in Trull Parish Archive by Mark McDermott, assisted by Tony Harding, Dave Taylor and Sarah Jeans.

Some more vernacular houses are referred to in Chapter 14, The Farms of Trull.

6 Church history

There may well have been a Saxon church in Trendle – as there was at neighbouring Wilton, where the distinctive 'long-and-short' masonry can still be seen. If there was, it would have been served by the missionary priests from Taunton Minster. But no documentary evidence or physical remains have been found.

Trull church was one of the chapels served by the canons of the Order of St Augustine from Taunton Priory before 1308. In that year a formal agreement was made between the Bishop of Bath & Wells, the Prior of Taunton Priory and the Vicar of St Mary Magdalene's, Master Simon de Lym. It laid down that the latter 'shall serve at his own cost by himself and his curates, the chapel of St Mary Magdalene of Taunton, of Trendle, of the Castle and of Fons S George (Wilton), in the sacraments and other Divine Offices of the Church; with this addition, that he shall find a priest constantly resident for the service at Trendle, as soon as the parishioners of the said chapel shall provide there a suitable house for the priest to live in'.

The house now known as Chantry Cottage (see page 16), beside the north gate of the churchyard, 'used to be known as Church Cottage, or the Clerk's Cottage, since the parish clerks formerly lived there. The original building seems to have been timber-framed, and could have been a priest's house before the Reformation'.[1] It is one of the oldest domestic buildings in the parish, and may well be on the site of the original priest's house referred to above.

The valuation of property and tithes belonging to the Priory made in 1534-5, shortly before the dissolution, contains the first direct reference to Trull as a parish. In the *Valor Ecclesiasticus* the sale of the 'Tithes of Corn of Hamwode, parcel of the parish of Trull' were £7 1s 4d. 'The Tithes of grain of Trulle with the oblations and other casualties' of the chapel were worth £6 0s 9d.

The Ministers' accounts, compiled not long after the dissolution of the Priory in 1539, gave the value of the 'farm of the Rectory' as £15. The right to the tithes of Trull passed to Humphrey Colles about 1543 when he bought the Barton Estate in Pitminster, and the owner of this estate was lay rector of Trull until 1936, and subsequently patron of the living. In the request to purchase of Humphrey Colles, it is said of 'the parsonage of Trull, parcel of the late Monastery of Taunton', that 'the trees growing about the scituacyon of the seyde parsonage & in hedges inclosynge lands parteyninge to the same wyll barely suffice to repayre the houses standynge upon the seyd scytuacyons and meynteyne the seyde hedges, therefore not valuid'.

In 1544 Henry VIII granted to Sir Francis Bryan and Matthew Coltehirste the 'Demayne Lands' of the late Priory. Some of these lands were in Trull parish. Among them were 'the Crofftes', which might be Crofts, the field to the east of Boxenhedge in Dipford, or Higher and Lower Longcroft to the north of Chilliswood; 'Somer Lease', possibly Summer Leaze Meadow west of Herswell Farm; and 'More Close', perhaps one of several fields in the area known as Trull Moor between Lower Comeytrowe and Galmington. But these demesne lands were scattered about in a number of parishes, and as the same field names may occur in more than one parish, it is impossible to identify with certainty those which were in Trull without research into the field names of several other parishes.

In 1623 at the Court of the Archdeacon of Taunton a presentment was made against Anthony Fuljames, to whom the tithes of Trull had been farmed out by the lay rector, and who was therefore responsible for the maintenance of the chancel of the church. This was said to be 'something decayed through want of couering', and Fuljames admitted 'that the same is not yet sufficiently repaired'.

There was evidently some conscientious objection among non-conformists to paying tithes, for in 1705 Peter Priest, a Quaker, was prosecuted by Smart Goodenough for not having paid his tithes for four years. Priest was a carrier from Taunton to London, and when he did not pay either the £16 due in tithes or the costs of the suit, he had 14 horses, worth £140, seized at their inn at Staines, 'and the innkeeper was obliged for their forthcoming before they were suffered to proceed on their journey'.

On the death of Francis Milner Newton in 1794, his daughter Josepha Sophia became impropriator of the tithes of Trull. She and her husband, Colonel Wheat, were stricter than their predecessors in exacting them, and the parishioners objected. In 1796 they sought counsel's advice as to 'whether they would be justified in resisting the Demand of Agistment Tithes in Respect of Grass that grows on meadow Ground after its having been mowed for Hay, which is called after-grass or after-math, and of Turnips sown after a Crop of Wheat called Wheat Eddish Turnips?' Counsel's opinion was that agistment tithe (money payment on grass or crops used for pasturing beasts) was not due on the after-grass, but that 'if the Turnips are drawn they are tythable in kind, if eaten on the ground undrawn an Agistment Tythe is due'. The following year the landholders sought the advice of another London lawyer on their liability for tithes, amongst other things for apples used to make cider and milk from their own cows, both for home consumption. The opinion was that both were tithable.

Mrs Josepha Sophia Wheat on her second marriage became Lady Cooper. The tithe apportionment of 1842 fixed the sums of money due to her in lieu of tithes in kind for every holding of land in the parish. The number of plots was 618, the total acreage 2,233, the number of land owners 42 and of occupiers 57, and the total value of the tithes £520.

The following list of incumbents has been compiled from many sources, most recently from the Clergy of the Church of England Database.[2] The dates given are the earliest for which evidence has been found, in the church registers or elsewhere.

1449   JOHN COKE
Parochial Chaplain. Robert Whyte, monk, was Anniversary Chaplain. He would have sung masses on the anniversaries of the deaths of those who left money for the purpose.

1468   JOHN FRENE
Chaplain of Trulle.

1500   THOMAS KEENE
Incumbent for 25 years. The parclose screens (see next Chapter) were erected in his memory.[3]

1533   JOHN SABYN
Chaplain of Trull in the *Valor Ecclesiasticus*. Stipend £6 13s 4d. He witnessed wills 1533-5. Described as curate on first page of register of baptisms in 1538.

1546   WILLIAM PESTON
John Alwyn of All Saints, Trull, bequeathed 1s to 'Will Preston, my curate'.

1560   RAFFE WYLKYNS
Curate, died December 1571. Bequeathed 6s 8d to churchwardens.

1572   ANTHONY KENE
Curate. Paid 6s 8d pa house rent to Churchwardens. Bequeathed 1s to them in 1580.

1582   WILLIAM BALL
Headed subscription lists with 1d.

1598   JOHN SHARPE
Curate.

1606   GISPERUS JONES
Office not stated.

1607   JOHN BROWN
Curate.

1620	**JOHN HARRIS**	

1620   JOHN HARRIS
       Curate.

1623   JOHN HARVEY
       Minister.

1633   ROGER DERBIE
       Curate. Signed as minister in 1639.

1659   BENJAMIN BERRY
       Curate. Ejected under the Act of Uniformity (see Chapter 11). Applied to return in 1672 but was refused.

1663   JOHN PARNELL
       Minister.

1664   MR SQUIBB
       Minister.

1666   THOMAS BABB
       Curate. Minister in 1671.

1673   JOHN HEWSEY
       'Minister of this parish was buried the 15th Day of June, 1675'.

1676   WILLIAM DENBAUD
       Curate.

1684   JOHN BALL
       Minister was buried 11th December 1684. 'Elizabeth his wife buried ye same day'.

1688   JOHN BAYLY
       Minister, attested overseers' accounts.

1698   HARRY BAYLIS
       Curate.

1700   JAMES HAYES
       Curate and preacher.

1707 PAT McDONALD
Curate.

1712 GEORGE ATWOOD
Minister. 16 marriages by licence and 5 by banns occurred from 1714 to 1727, all between couples of whom neither was resident in the parish. Atwood signed registers until 1747 and his handwriting continued until 1752.

1752 JOHN STIBBS
Perpetual curate.

1761 JAMES HURLY
Minister. James Hurly junior acted as curate.

1785 JAMES HURLY jnr.
Began to sign as minister instead of curate.

1788 MICHAEL DICKSON
Perpetual curate, then minister. Signed registers 1807-1836. Francis Hunt Clapp was curate 1787-1797. John Gale was curate 1797-1807. In 1842 Revd John Gale was living in the house called 'The Old Vicarage', then owned by John Clitsome.

1837 JOHN GEB
Minister. Thomas Tudball was assistant stipendiary curate at £50 p.a. 1842-45.

1845 GILBERT H WEST
Incumbent. LA Cliffe was Curate 1846-50.

1854 HENRY CHARLES SELLER
Incumbent – see Chapter 18.

1857 ROBERT JOHN GOULD
Incumbent

1858 WILLIAM JEFFERYS ALLEN, JP
Incumbent, lived at Gatchell House. Annual value of living £90. Frederick Lillington, living at Dipford, was assistant stipendiary curate at £40 pa.

1863 HENRY CHARLES SELLER
Incumbent again. Annual value of living £130 in 1866. He lived in the house now

called 'The Old Vicarage' and seems to have been the first incumbent to be given the courtesy title of vicar.

1882 JOHN HENRY SOUTHAM
Vicar, lived at 'The Old Vicarage'. He was a strong supporter of the Temperance Movement.

1906 RICHARD YERBURGH BONSEY
Vicar, having previously been the incumbent at Pitminster. Was first to live in what is now 'The Old Rectory', built in 1908.

1914 KENNETH WILLIAM PRIDGIN TEALE
Vicar, having previously been a missionary in New Zealand.

1919 MARTIN LEONARD WINTERTON
Wrote All Saints Trull *Brief History of the Parish Church* in 1933.

1946 CHARLES WILLIAM TREVELYAN
Discovered in the parish chest many of the documents referred to in this book, including the earliest register, the 16th century churchwardens' accounts and the church seating plans of 1569 and 1635. Presented the bound volumes of the *Parish Magazine* to the parish as a leaving present.

1958 HAROLD WILLIAM TREMLETT STAMP
Moved here after 10 years service as vicar of Hemyock. His involvement with Trull School was particularly valued.

1961 DEREK COURTNEY EVANS
Previously curate at St Mary Magdalene's, Taunton for four years. Served as Rural Dean for part of his ministry in Trull.

1978 RICHARD ERNEST BALLARD
First rector of Trull with Angersleigh. Much involved with Queen's College and moved on to Wells Cathedral School.

1982 JOHN MISKIN PRIOR
Very experienced parish priest. His wife Phyllis died in 1985, during his ministry here. He was also Rural Dean for several years.

1992 ROSS HATHWAY
Born and ordained in Australia. First 'Evangelical' incumbent.

(Left to right) Top row: Richard Yerburgh Bonsey, Martin Leonard Winterton, Charles William Trevelyan. Middle row: Harold William Tremlett Stamp, Derek Courtney Evans, Richard Ernest Ballard. Bottom row: John Miskin Prior, Ross Hathway.

2003   ADRIAN YOUINGS
Was briefly rector only of Trull, following pastoral reorganisation. But Joint Benefice with Angersleigh was restored on appeal. Appointed to Archdeacon of Bath 2017. Curates were Mark Wallace 2008-12 and Mark Close 2014-17.

2018   ANDREW WADSWORTH
Ordained in 2001 and served his curacy at St Andrew's, Plymouth before church planting Grace Church Highlands from Christ Church Cockfosters in north London in 2007. Moved to Trull with Angersleigh in autumn 2018 prior to the upheavals of Covid-19.

Imogen and Jonathan Ball were job-sharing curates from 2021. Ordained in 2022 by the Bishop of Bath and Wells in All Saints church, the first recorded ordination here (see photo below). Imogen became the first woman priest to be on the staff of the Joint Benefice. See also first paragraph on page 144.

(Left to right) Adrian Youings, Andrew Wadsworth (second left)

References
1. CW Green, *Trull and Staplehay with an eye on the past*, Trull School (1993) p.6.
2. Clergy of the Church of England Database: www.theclergydatabase.org.uk.
3. Rev ML Winterton, *Brief History of the Parish Church by the Vicar*, The Phoenix Press (1937).

7 All Saints Church

The frontispiece of this book is a photograph of the church taken in 1860, when the walls were stuccoed and lime washed. It seems likely that until 1863 it had always been the practice to stucco or rough-cast the church (see references to expenditure on maintenance in the next chapter). Not for nothing has the nationwide Victorian church restoration been nicknamed 'The Great Scrape'! In the 1980s, when an appeal had to be launched to pay for the extensive repointing of the tower, our church architect recommended rendering the church again (as at Angersleigh) to protect the stonework. The PCC were horrified at the suggestion!

The stone used by the medieval builders was mostly grey Triassic sandstone and hard marl, possibly quarried at Rumwell, with some red sandstone of the same geological age. The window framings and mullions and parts of the buttresses are of freestone from Ham Hill, and this Ham stone has been re-used for repair work in the walls, together with some Lias limestone. A great deal of re-facing was done with Blackdown chert, probably in the 19th century.

The base of the tower, built in the late 13th century,[1] is the oldest surviving part of the church. The west window is of three stepped lancet lights, and unlike most medieval churches there has never been a west door.

The south arcade dates from the latter part of the 14th century and the north arcade and aisle from the middle of the 15th century, but the battlemented south aisle was probably re-built early in the 16th century. The chancel opens to the aisles on either side of it by single arches of a late Perpendicular style. The north doorway has a shallow porch terminating in a buttress. It is earlier than the aisle, and may have been partly re-used from a nave of the 13th century. The vestry, added in 1812, is built of brick plastered over in imitation of the stonework. The nave has a waggon roof with three purlins and small bosses, and the aisles have lean-to roofs with richly carved bosses.

The church is famous for its carved woodwork. The rood screen has fan vaulting and cornice of a kind more commonly found in Devon than in Somerset, and may have been made by men trained in one of the Exeter workshops. There is now no tracery, but each bay once had a central mullion. An unusual feature is that the screen does not, and never did, continue across the aisles as is usual in churches without chancel arches.

The staircase to the rood loft (a narrow gallery on top of the screen) is a very steep and narrow one in the thickness of the north arcade, but the entrance to it is now blocked. The shape of the entrances onto the screen on either side can still be seen.

The parclose screens in the aisles never carried lofts. The tracery is of a type very rare in Somerset, and more like that commonly found in East Anglia. According to Revd ML Winterton, a former vicar,[2] they were erected to the memory of Thomas Keene, incumbent here 1500-1525. Unfortunately he does not give his source for this information, and no other record has been found. Over the head of the doorway in the north aisle screen is the following inscription:

Interpretation has proved to be very difficult. The first name may be 'Tomaes (Thomas) le helyer' and the wording on the lower image appears to be 'Joan Kien'. The Trull churchwardens' accounts for 1537-8 refer to a payment for a knell for 'Jone Kene', who must therefore have died in that year. She may have been the Joan Kien whose name appears on the screen, but this is by no means certain.

Nikolaus Pevsner described the pulpit as: 'Something unique in the county, a wooden pulpit with undamaged figures of the saints' (see photo below). The large carved figures represent, from left to right, St John the Evangelist holding the cup with a serpent flying out of it; St Gregory in papal tiara with two crowns; St Augustine (of Hippo) (or St Ambrose); St Jerome; and St Ambrose (or St Augustine). These figures are said to have been hidden under the floor to save them from destruction by the puritans. The small figures between the large ones have been defaced. From the church seating plans of 1569 and 1635 it is clear that the pulpit was formerly immediately to the west of the middle pillar of the north arcade. Scars in the pillar bear this out, as does the fact that the moulding of the partition between the pews stops short of the pillar. The pulpit was probably placed in its present position during the restoration of 1863.

Much of the seating is ancient, the plan of 1569 is believed to be the oldest in the country.[3] In Georgian times the benches on the south side at the front of the nave were replaced by box pews (see drawing on page 41 dated 1846). Medieval Gothic was then considered 'primitive' compared with the new classical style. These box pews may also have brought in valuable pew rent for the church, and provided privacy for the wealthier parishioners.

Most of the benchends are carved with geometrical designs and conventional fruit and foliage. One of them is dated 1530, but they show little trace of Renaissance influence. Five of them represent figures with prominent legs showing below their vestments. One of these is now in the north aisle and the others separated from one another in the south aisle, but originally they were probably together, and may have depicted a procession to the font. They seem to represent a clerk carrying the cross, a taperer with a candle, a subdeacon with a crismatory, a deacon with the book, and the officiant in a cope. Some linen-fold panelling at the west end of the north aisle is unlike most of the seating, and has the inscription: 'SIMON WARMAN, MAKER OF THYS WORKE, ANNO D(OMI)NI 1560', and above: 'JOHN WAYE CLARKE HERE'. Warman carved many of the benchends, as explained in our *Church Guide*.[4]

The inscription to John Waye is not integral with the panelling which is inscribed to Simon Warman, and seems to have been taken from another feature in the church.

The east window of the chancel still contains much medieval glass, but has been extensively restored. The famous 'Dragon Window' on the south side of the chancel (see below), which depicts SS Michael, Margaret of Antioch, and George, each slaying a dragon, is mostly medieval but the figure of St Margaret is modern. The stained glass has been dated to the late 14th century by the plate armour worn by Michael and George.

In 1885 the window on the east side of the door in the north aisle was restored through the generosity of Mrs Byng Paget, much of it with 15th century glass which had been 'stored away in a box in the blanket room' for 23 years. Five of the windows in the aisles illustrate the canticle *Te Deum Laudamus* from the Matins service in the 1662 *Book of Common Prayer*.

By the early years of the 19th century the church fabric was clearly in a poor state. George Trevelyan, Archdeacon of Taunton, after his visitation on 23rd November 1818, gave the following directions to the minister and churchwardens of Trull:

'To sink the ground surrounding the external walls of the Building as nearly as possible to the level of the Church floor and to form proper gutters to convey the water therefrom –
To repair the wood work of the window on the south side of the Tower –
To employ an able and experienced plumber to examine the roof on the south side of the Church and to repair the same according to his opinion –
The Necessary belonging to the Church house to be repaired and no nuisance suffered in future to be committed in the Churchyard – and the Churchyard fence to be repaired –
To repair and level or new lay the pavement of the Church where requiring such repair or new laying –
To provide a new Bier and Bier Cloth, the tables of Commandments, and a Table of 'Degrees of Marriage' –
To repair the ceiling of Belfry and the floors of such pews in the Church as may require repair –
To Provide a new Bible, a new Book of Common Prayer, and a new Surplice for the Minister, also proper Cushions for the use of the Communicants at the altar –
I beg leave to recommend (if it be possible) that the doors of Cottages opening into the Churchyard be stopped, and doors opened for the use of the Cottagers on the opposite side –
To enjoin the Person who has the care of the Church to open all the casements in the windows thereof on every dry day, when the wind is not too rough – as nothing conduces so much to the keeping the Church in good repair, and wholesome for the use of the Congregation as a free circulation of dry air –
Lastly to direct that the rubbish of all kinds be removed from the Church and Churchyard, and the former kept well swept and clean.'

The watercolour of the church in 1851 by J. W. Archer, picture opposite, well illustrates the neglect identified by the Archdeacon. It is reproduced by kind permission of Tom Mayberry.

In 1863 a faculty was granted to 'repair and improve the parish church of Trull'. This included 'the taking down of the communion table and rails, the pulpit, reading desk, organ gallery, font and pews, and erecting new ones; also the repair and restoration of the floors of the saide Church and chancel'.

The replacement of the pulpit was bitterly opposed by the churchwardens, and we may be thankful to them that we do not have a Victorian pulpit in the church today. The scurrilous broadsheet *Selly's Dogmas* printed in 1871 (see page 109) shows how long the controversy between vicar and churchwardens lasted. The box pews were taken down about 1863, but the font was not replaced until November 1869. The new font was given by the Vibart family of Chilliswood. It is not known what happened to the medieval font.

The gallery mentioned on page 42 was erected by Robert Mattock at the west end of the nave in 1786 to accommodate the singers and an accompanying string and wind band,[5] in typical 18th century fashion, but in 1827 Mr H Bryceson was paid to build a 'finger and Barrel Organ' in the gallery. The singers received new music books and there was a salaried organist who in 1834 was instructed to be responsible for the performance and good conduct of the choir, including a weekly choir practice. West gallery music went out of fashion in Victorian England under the influence of the High Church movement and in 1889 the Trull gallery was taken down and the organ moved to the present position and 'improved'. In 1968 the ringing chamber was created in the west tower, with a choir vestry below which is now also used as a refuge for parents with small children during church services.

The church floor, or part of it, was paved with tiles in medieval times. One of these tiles is preserved in the Museum of Somerset. It is one of a set of four made in the late 15th or early 16th century. A tile of the same set at Poundisford Park has the letters 'AVE MARIA I H S'. The slate slabs in the chancel (complete with fossils) date from 2007, when the choir pews were replaced with chairs to create an open space for the music group and other activities.

During the work a medieval piscina, for washing the priest's hands and the communion vessels, was uncovered in the south wall of the south chapel. This suggests that this area was a chantry chapel, where a priest would recite masses for the souls of the dead, to shorten their time in purgatory. A religious fraternity dedicated to the Virgin Mary, which enabled both men and women to share the benefits and cost of employing a chantry priest, is recorded in Trull in the first half of the 16th century, but may have been set up earlier.[6] The piscina was associated with an altar in the south chapel which may have been used by this fraternity. In 1547, during the Protestant Reformation of Edward VI's reign, all such fraternities were dissolved by Act of Parliament, and it may have been then that the piscina became redundant and was blocked up.

In 2002 the Victorian pine south door was replaced by the present glass-panelled one, as a memorial to William Stansell, churchwarden for many years, head of the building firm and a generous benefactor to the church.

The church has a peal of six bells. The earliest was cast by Roger Semson of Ash Priors in about 1550. Two were cast in 1660. The largest, the tenor, was added in 1860, and the final two in 1887 to commemorate Queen Victoria's Golden Jubilee. The frame was made and installed by John Kebby of Broomfield in 1769. The bells were thoroughly retuned and rehung in 1933.

The oldest surviving memorial in the church is a stone one on the floor at the east end of the south aisle, dating from 1641. All the memorials, on the floor, walls and in the windows, are described and illustrated in Cyril Green's comprehensive booklet, published posthumously in 2008 and available from the Church Office or the Parish Archive.[7] The chest tomb of Edward Berrie dating from the 17th century is just outside the south porch, and is a listed monument in its own right.

The timber-framed building shown below stood on the western edge of the churchyard and was drawn by Edward Jeboult when it was being demolished in 1886. This was the former parish Church House which was originally used for fund-raising celebrations known as 'church ales' and was an early equivalent of a village hall or parish room.

SKETCH OF THE ANCIENT CHURCH-HOUSE AT TRULL - REMOVAL OF THE ROOF

AN EARLY WOOD-FRAMED HOUSE IN THE ·S·W· CORNER OF THE CHURCHYARD
Edward Jeboult 1886

A church house is referred to frequently from 1526 onwards in the surviving churchwardens' accounts for Trull, including annual payments of 2s 6d rent, possibly to the lord of the manor. The churchwardens received 'of Thomas Whithorne for the churchhose sollere [solar/chamber] iijs. [3 shillings]' in 1582 and 'of John Lane the younger for the churchhouse soller iijs. iiijd.' in 1584, which may refer to hire for private use. The Church House probably dated from the 15th century but may have been rebuilt in 1546-7 when an 'old house' was taken down and a new one constructed. It had a thatched roof which was possibly renewed in 1573 when 11s 4d was paid 'to the helyer', a roofer, for 'mending of the churche howsse'.

When church houses fell out of use for their original purposes in the 17th century the builings were sometimes used for other functions, such as alehouses, almshouses or schools. Trull Church House was used to accommodate a school set up in 1755 by the trustees of the John Wyatt Charity (see page 95). The Trull tithe map of 1843 shows a long, narrow structure on the western edge of the churchyard, which according to the accompanying schedule (dated 1842) consisted of a cottage and a schoolroom, owned by the parish officers and occupied by Richard Penny and others. The school moved to the present site in 1875 and the former Church House, possibly with one or more adjoining cottages, was finally demolished in 1886.

The churchyard was further enlarged in 1904, when the site of the Poor House near the north-east corner of the church (see page 65) was taken, together with part of Lady Land; and again in the 1950s when more of Lady Land was enclosed. Lady Land was named after Our Lady (the Virgin Mary) and was owned by the fraternity described on page 49 as a source of income. The Lady Lawn development on the remainder of Lady Land in 1987 meant that the churchyard could not be extended any further. The walnut tree was planted on Easter Day 1989, in memory of Clem Toy.

Beside the path from the church to Chantry Cottage, under a yew tree, are the stocks which date to the 18th century or earlier. They were last used in 1855, when William Blake, who was church warden at the time, caused a drunken Thomas Trout, who had disturbed services in the church, to be placed in them.[8]

The surviving churchwardens' accounts show that the church had a clock at least as early as 1530-31. In 1906 the present church clock, with four-foot dials facing north, south and west, was provided by a bequest in memory of Caroline Norman. It strikes the quarters on four bells and the hours on the tenor. It was originally wound by hand twice a week but is now electrified. The clock was regilded in 2023 as part of the church building project funded by a very generous legacy from Ruth Pewtress, who required it to be spent on the fabric of the church. Other planned improvements over the next few years are new sound, lighting and heating systems; an accessible toilet in the choir vestry; a more welcoming south porch; a new bell-frame and tower roof access; repairs and retuning of the bells themselves at Loughborough Foundry (see below) and a memorial garden in the churchyard.

References
1. N Pevsner, *The Buildings of England: South and West Somerset* (1958) p.325.
2. Rev ML Winterton, *Brief History of the Parish Church by the Vicar* (1937), p.9.
3. M McDermott, 'The Trull church seating plan of 1569' in *Somerset & Dorset Notes & Queries*, XXXIX, Pt. 400, Sept. 2024, No. 64, p.467. Also transcription on website www.sdnq.org.uk.
4. D Archer, *What to look for in All Saints Church Trull*, set of five leaflets dated 2013 available in All Saints Church or from the Church Office.
5. MB McDermott, 'West Gallery at All Saints' Church, Trull' in *Somerset & Dorset Notes & Queries* (March 1997), pp. 89-92.
6. Dunning & McDermott, *Church Accounts*, p.238.
7. CW Green MA, *Trull Church Memorials* (2008).
8. RJE Bush, *A Taunton Diary 1787-1987* (1988) p.42.

8 Church revenue and expenditure

Wills of the early 16th century show that even the poorest left money to the church.[1] Anthony Phillypps, who died in 1535, left 'our lady servys of Trull – my beste cote – Alsolyn lyght ijd. – hyghe crosse lyghte ijs. – torches ijd.'. This adds up to 2s 4d, not counting the coat. He also left 2d to Wells Cathedral, and as his total estate was only 13s 8d, his wife fared badly. Richer men left larger sums for similar purposes. Robarte Smythe bequeathed 'To Almes for my soule' £6 13s 4d, and to 'the seagninge (? ceiling) of the church of Trull' £6.

A remarkable range of parish records survives for Trull, including two parallel sets of accounts surviving from the first half of the 16th century.[2] One consists of churchwardens' accounts from 1525-6 until 1547-8, plus part of an account for 1550; and the other is a set of accounts of a religious guild or lay fraternity, dedicated to the Virgin Mary, from 1525-6 until 1549-50.

The churchwardens' accounts show that much of their income came from church ales that were festivities which took place in the Church House. There was expenditure not only on the church itself but on the Church House, a well (which was a roofed structure), a stable and a bench and fencing in the churchyard. There was also a chamber (possibly in the Church House) for which John Saben or Sabyn, the curate, paid rent to the churchwardens. The accounts also provide insights into the life of the church both before and during the Henrician Reformation. The church fittings included a rood loft (above the rood screen) which was renewed in the later 1530s at considerable expense by a wood carver named John Beny or Bynny, and there are also references to Our Lady's light, a trendle or corona (hoop) with candles attached for All Hallows night, a Lent cloth (presumably over a crucifix) and the use of frankincense, and in 1542-3 a payment was made for 'dressynge of the ymagis' (dressing the images). The accounts also reveal that the church had a clock at least as early as 1530-31 (although in 1532-3 15s was paid for 'making' a clock), and also an organ on which 12s was spent in 1539-40, whilst in 1544-5 2s 2d was paid to 'Nycolas the organ maker', perhaps for repairs.

Until 1476 burials of inhabitants of Trull (which was a chapelry) had taken place in the lay cemetery of the Augustinian priory in Taunton, but from that year burials were permitted in the churchyard in Trull.[3] The churchwardens had to make payments to the prior for permission to do this, for example in 1532-3 they paid £14 to the prior 'for the beryall off [of] the chyrch yerde'. When the priory was dissolved in 1539 by Henry VIII (now Head of the Church of England after the separation from Rome earlier in the 1530s) the wardens paid a lump sum which brought these payments to an end.

The dissolution of the monasteries in the 1530s was part of the Henrician Reformation which also affected Trull in other ways. In 1538, for example, all parishes were obliged to keep a register of baptisms, marriages and burials, which had to be kept in a locked coffer (the purchase of a lock for a coffer is referred to in the Trull accounts), and a copy of a *Holy Bible* in English had to be placed in each church. Thus in 1540-41 the Trull wardens paid 18s 4d to meet half the cost of a *Holy Bible*, the other half was met by Simon Fayrwyll, and the wardens then paid 4d for a chain and 'dressing' of the *Holy Bible*.

Trull is referred to as a parish in the Valor Ecclesiasticus in 1535. The Valor refers to John Sabyn as a chaplain, implying that Trull was still a chapelry subordinate to the vicar of St Mary in Taunton and to the prior of Taunton priory, under the terms of the Ordination of the Vicarage of St Mary in 1308. A more crucial turning-point in the emergence of Trull as a parish seems to have been the dissolution of the priory in 1539. It not only enabled the Trull churchwardens to pay a composition to establish permanent burial rights in Trull, but also enabled Humphrey Colles to acquire (in c.1543) the Barton estate (a former priory estate) in Corfe and Pitminster with the right to the tithes of Trull, formerly payable to the priory. Thereafter the owners of the estate and tithes were lay rectors of Trull, with authority as patron to nominate a perpetual curate. The latter had a lifelong tenure, which a mere chaplain or curate did not.

The lay fraternity, whose wardens kept their own separate accounts relating to 'the store' (i.e. fund or property) of Our Lady of Trull, is sometimes referred to as a brotherhood or as 'the service' of Our Lady. This kind of organization was a poor man's chantry, although in this instance the benefits were not confined to men. The wardens employed a chantry priest to perform masses for deceased members of the fraternity in order to reduce the length of time their souls would spend in purgatory. John Yordeyn is referred to in 1539-40 and 1541-2, and then Humphrey Bere who was succeeded in 1542-3 by William Hawkyns who was still in post in 1547.

The fraternity wardens' sources of income, to meet the cost of the priest's stipend and other expenses, included the profits of ales. The Rood Mass ales were especially profitable but smaller sums were also raised at All Hallows' ales. Other sources were gifts of ale (presumably for consumption at ales or funeral wakes) and various sums of money and personal items which were often given as bequests. For example, Antony Phillypps left 'my best cote' to Our Lady's service of Trull in 1535 and Ede Babbe left 'my best kyrtell saving owne' in 1543. The wardens even acquired an anvil and tools which they were able to hire out.

Further income came from various properties which could be used productively or rented out. These included a house in Taunton known as Our Lady's house and pieces of land such as Yard (or Half Yard) in Pitminster parish, Rixham Mead in Bishops Hull, Luscombe (or

Liscombe) near the present Queen's Drive, and Lady Land immediately to the north of Trull churchyard. Parts of Lady Land were incorporated into the churchyard at various dates and most of the remainder is now occupied by the modern housing development known as Ladylawn.

The Trull fraternity continued to be active until all chantries were dissolved by an Act of parliament passed in 1547, at the beginning of Edward VI's reign, during which a more Protestant version of the Reformation took place. Although the surviving Trull churchwardens' accounts for this reign are incomplete, they reveal that in 1550 the altars in the church were taken down, which must have included that used by the chantry priest that was possibly in the south chapel of the church where a blocked piscina has been exposed (see page 44). In the same year the accounts refer to the defacing of a cross and the setting up of the Ten Commandments in the church, possibly replacing medieval wall paintings. Following the dissolution of the Trull fraternity its former properties came to be administered by the churchwardens and the Trull Parish Lands Charity, now renamed the Trull Parish Lands Community Fund (see Chapter 13).

After 1550 the next churchwardens' accounts to survive date from 1571, during Elizabeth I's reign, so there is no record of how the parish was affected by the short-lived return to Romanism during Mary Tudor's reign. The support which had been given to the lay fraternity, however, suggests that Trull parishioners were conservative in their religious outlook.

The churchwardens' accounts for 1571-1588 and for 1692-1916 are also preserved in the Somerset Heritage Centre. The Elizabethan account book is particularly valuable as a source of social history. At this time there were three churchwardens each year, and they did not normally hold office for more than a year at a time. The income came from bequests and gifts, house rent from the curate, the letting of the upper room in the Church House, the sale of the grass of the churchyard and occasionally of faggots. Payments for the ringing of the knells ceased in 1580. Between 1581 and 1588 William Palmer contributed £37 8s 3d from two to six payments being made each year. The amounts are so variable as to preclude their being for rents, and it must be concluded that he was the benefactor at whose expense the building operations described later in this chapter were undertaken.

In 1573, a chalice was changed into a communion cup, which had become necessary after the Reformation when the practice of taking communion in both kinds (bread and wine) began. The chalice was evidently melted down and less silver used to make the cup, for the accounts are credited with 7s 2d. This cup is no longer in the church, the earliest surviving piece of plate being a flagon with the date letter for 1731.

The expenses were many and various. There were constant repairs to the bells, and a certain amount of money was given in charity. Items such as the following occur. 'Item payd to fower poor maimed souldiers of Flanders – 6d' and 'Item payd to the pore at Brysto – 12d'. The latter was probably in response to an appeal or 'brief', sent round to meet some special emergency. In 1577 and in 1587 the parish contributed to the expenses of the visits of 'my lord bysshope of Canterburye at Tanton'.

So much work was done on the fabric of the church in 1586-7 that it is hardly surprising that the churchwardens' accounts end, 'So we have layed out £3 6s 10d more than we have received'. That year the clock house was repaired or rebuilt, and £1 13s paid 'to William Prieste for the clock'. This might have been sufficient to buy a clock at that date. If so, it replaced an earlier one, as repairs to a clock are mentioned in previous years. The same year the tower was rough cast, the sand being brought from Bathpool Mill. A major work of reconstruction or extension must have been carried out between 1586 and 1589 as the following analysis of building expenses shows:

		£	s	d
1586–7	11 load of stones	3	8	4
	1 load of flagstones		3	4
	Carriage of stone	1	13	0
	Lime		16	8
	2 putt loads of sand, including carriage		5	6
	Iron		3	8
	Nails		1	1
	18 lb. of lead		1	11
	1 peck of scredes [small pebbles]			2
	Timber		8	8
	TOTAL FOR MATERIALS AND CARRIAGE	7	2	4
	TOTAL FOR ABOUT 187 DAYS LABOUR	5	3	1
	TOTAL BUILDING EXPENSES	12	5	5
1587–8	Timber (including carriage)	1	13	9
	3 sacks of lime		2	3
	Nails etc.		8	4
	TOTAL FOR MATERIALS AND CARRIAGE	2	4	2
	TOTAL FOR LABOUR.	2	5	9
	TOTAL BUILDING EXPENSES	4	9	11
1588–9	2000 Tiling Stones (including carriage)		13	4
	Ovis [eaves?] stones		2	6
	Carriage		3	-
	Carriage of sand		1	-
	6 sacks of lime		4	6

Laths		2	10
5 ½ pecks of tiling pins		3	8
Nails		5	3
TOTAL FOR MATERIALS AND CARRIAGE	1	11	7
TOTAL FOR LABOUR	1	11	2
TOTAL BUILDING EXPENSES	3	2	9

John Shut was the master mason, and he received 1s a day, while his three men worked for less. A skilled man's wage was 10d a day, while the ordinary labourer usually received 8d. The masons finished their work in 1586-7. The following year Christopher Pulman, the regular carpenter, and his man were employed in felling and sawing, needing other men to help them. In the third year of this building operation it was John Heliar alone who did the tiling.

The amount of material used would probably have been sufficient to build either an aisle, or an extension of the chancel, or the upper part of the tower, assuming it was all used on the church; it might have been on the church house. Both aisles were in existence in 1569, as the church seating plan proves, and from their architectural features it seems highly improbable that they were rebuilt as late as 1586–9. Dr FC Eeles has suggested that the rebuilding of the chancel came later than the main 15th century rebuilding. But the chancel should have been the responsibility of the rector, not of the churchwardens. Another possibility is that the upper part of the tower was built or rebuilt at this time, but it seems unlikely that the tower would have been rough cast in 1586-7 before the major work of reconstruction was finished, and the two thousand tiles bought in 1588-9 would not have been required for the tower roof. On the other hand, 2s 10d was paid to John Bull, the blacksmith, in 1587-8 for twelve pounds of iron 'that stayeth up the penicles'.

The following items from the accounts for 1588-9 are worth noting:

Item for payd John Hull & George Potter for carringe in of the stones of the crosse	06d
Item payed Hughe Lome for taking out of the led	02d
Item payed Thomas Bull making cleane of ye crosse	01d

John Bull was paid 2s for the iron that was in the cross. It seems probable that a cross formerly in the churchyard was set up within the church or that its stones were re-used. Page 22 of the first account book, transcribed below, gives part of the payments for 1577 when the bells were rung for Queen Elizabeth I.

Item paid unto Xpoffer [Christopher] Pullman for a planke & the setting therof upon the church' dowre	06d

Item paid for oyle agynst alhallondaye [All Saints Day] for the belles		02d
Item paid at the last vicitacion at Taunton	06s	06d
Item paid unto Mr. Anthonye o[u]r curat towards his chargis to cary the Regestor bock to Melverton [a residence of the Archdeacon of Taunton]		06d
Item paid for oyle for the bells [inserted by caret] & candells to gyve light to the Ryngers that Ronge for the Reioysynge of the quene maiests Raigne whiche I praye God longe to contynew &c.		03d
Item paid for a breakfast for the Ryngers at Nycholas Heryngs being in Number 15 men	02s	10d
Item paid unto Nycholas Heryng for his Fee to see the bell is in order	03s	00d
Item paid unto John Bull & for 4 steripes to make fast a pee [a weight] uppon the fowrthe bell & for a plat for to sett upon the wheale & nayles		10d
Item for the churche house Rent	02s	06d

The churchwardens' accounts for 1702-3, the year Queen Anne was crowned, show that by this time the whole income was derived from ownership of property in Taunton, Bishops Hull and Lowton as well as in Trull. The following extracts give some idea of how the income was spent.

	£	s	d
Pd The Land Tax in Hilbishops	0	09	06
Pd The Clarke his sallary	2	00	00
Pd For bread and wine for Easter communion	0	05	00
Pd Att visitation for a diner	0	11	06
Pd For fileing ye register and proclamation	0	02	00
Gave ringers the crowing [crowning] queen	0	06	00
Pd Foull Smith for Aulling ye bells	0	00	06
Pd For half a hundred of reed the house in Taunton	0	10	06
Pd Thacher Laying it up & spars	0	06	08
Pd For Ire gare [iron gear] aboute ye bells	0	02	11
Pd For Lords rent for ye parish land	0	14	03
Gave Ringers ye Fifth of November	0	15	09
Pd The Masons for 8 days worke about Church & ye Churchhouse	0	16	00
Pd For Lime & stone about ye Church	0	11	09
Pd For glasing ye Church Windows	0	13	08
Pd The Constable for money due for carrying vagrants thorow ye county	0	04	06
Pd The Constable for repaireing of Yeawh bridge*	0	05	00¾
Pd For washing ye surplis	0	03	00
Pd For mending ye Coffer & Key for ye Locke for ye Clarke to keep ye pulpit cloth and books	0	00	08
Pd The waywardens' warrant	0	02	06

*A bridge over the River Yeo in north Somerset. There was a disastrous storm in 1703, and this probably destroyed the bridge. A county rate was levied to meet the cost of rebuilding.

The accounts for 1702-3 end as follows:

	£	s	d
The Summ Disbusted	19	16	02¼
The Summ Recd.	36	15	00
Due for ye parish	16	18	09¾

The accounts for 1838-9, the year Queen Victoria was crowned, show a large increase in income and in expenses. Most receipts were from property, the rent of Totterdell's Farm bringing in £20 14s a half year. The letting of the room over the school brought in £1 and the grass of the churchyard 5s.

The following extracts from the payments show that the entries were less detailed than those of earlier accounts.

	£	s	d
Ringers 29th May		10	6
Do Coronation Queen Victoria		10	6
Sacrament Wine	1	4	0
March 9th paid County Stock	9	3	10¾
Clark's Salary	1	0	0
Mr Atton's Bill		11	10
Mr Long's Bill for Pinnacles on Tower	6	0	0
Samuel Billets Bill	5	7	3
Mr Westcotts Bill	6	5	3
Mr Ray's Bill	3	0	0
Bill for repairing Totterdells Barn		19	8
Organists Salary	12	0	0
Stuckey for Singing	1	1	0

References
1. FW Weaver, ed, *Wells Wills* (1890), pp. 174-6; F Brown, ed, *Somersetshire Wills* (1889), iii, p. 61; v. 68.
2. SHC, DD/CT 77 transcribed in Dunning and McDermott, *Church Accounts*, pp. 235-303.
3. RJE Bush, *The Book of Taunton* (1977), p. 39.

9 Life of Nicholas Heryng

Nicholas Heryng was presumably born before 1538, as there is no mention of his baptism in the earliest parish register beginning in that year. In 1561 the entry 'Jan 23. Nicholas Herryng was wedded' is the only one in this early marriage register, which omits the name of the wife. She may have been Agnes Heryng, who sat in the back row of seats in the south side of the nave in Trull church, according to the seating plan of 1569. Their first daughter Joan was baptised two months after their marriage, and two more daughters, Isabel and 'Anys' (Agnes), were baptised in 1563 and 1565.

In 1569 Nicholas Heringe is listed as one of the eight 'ablemen' of North Trendle Tithing. He was a 'pekeman' (pikeman) in the armed force raised because of the danger of invasion by the Spaniards in the time of Queen Elizabeth I. The other ablemen of the same tithing were archers and bill-men. He would not have been expected to go outside the county except in a serious emergency, and would have received 8d a day when there was a muster. The penalty for non-attendance was ten days' imprisonment or a fine of 40s, so we may assume he did not fail to go for training when called upon.

In 1575 Nicholas Heryng and John Woodland were paid ¾d for 'kepyng of the bells', the next year they received 4s and the partnership continued for nine years. After this Nicholas Heryng looked after the bells for 4s a year until 1588-9. He also bought the oil, and the ringers were paid through him. When any major repairs to the bells were needed he helped John Farmer with them. For three-and-a-half days' work 'at taske' he was paid at the rate of 10d a day, but for another day's work he only got 8d. He did other odd jobs such as cutting grass and 'caryage of barris and postes', and on one occasion he paid 1s 4d and another 1s for the grass of the churchyard.

The churchwardens received 'of the gyfte of Anys Heryng … 11s 1d' in 1575-6. She probably died between this date and 1584-5, for in that year Joan, the eldest daughter of Nicholas, received 'for meat and drinke while the bells were a mending 17s 9d'. Joan again supplied food and drink for men working in the church building in 1588-89. It may be presumed that Nicholas lived close to the church, and it seems possible that he had quarters in the Church House, for 15 men were present at a breakfast for the ringers in 1577-8 'at Nicholas Heryngs' so that he must have had an unusually large room in which to entertain them. He may have been sexton or done some other work in return for lodging. 1583-4 is the only year in which it is recorded that he paid 6d rent.

Nicholas was churchwarden in 1580-81. The date of his death is not known. His life is probably typical of many village men in the days of Queen Elizabeth I, and we may think of him sitting in his seat between Thomas Kene and Roberte Pears in the second pew of the north aisle of Trull church regularly every Sunday, while his women folk sat separately at the back of the church.

10 Women in the sixteenth century

Women seem to have had more standing in the days of Queen Elizabeth I than they had in the following century. The church seating plan of 1569 gives the women of the parish by name, whereas the plan of 1635 lists them as wives of the men. In both cases they sat apart from their husbands, either in the south aisle or behind the 'Crosse Alley' between the north and south doors.

Jone Gybbbens of Trull, whose will was proved in January 1535, died not long after her husband, the residue of whose estate had been left to her. She gave instructions, common at the time, to be buried in the 'holly grave of Trull', and left 4d to Wells Cathedral, 1s 8d to the services of Our Lady at Trull, three 'kows', one to each of three male relatives, and a 'yerling' to another, and 'my peace of clothe half to Hary Gebons, halfe to Cristofer Gebons'. Other bequests included 1s to every godchild and 1s 8d to 'Sir Sabyn my gostly father', the curate at Trull who was one of the witnesses of the will.

Ede Babbe, who made her will in January 1543, left to the services of Our Lady at Trull 'my beste kyrtell saving owne'. The best kirtle and other apparel went to Joan Babbe, wife of John Babbe. To her daughter Alice she left apparel, bedding, household stuff and £10 in money, with the proviso that, if she died before being married, then £6 of the money was to be paid to a priest for one year to sing for the souls of Robert Babbe and Ede his wife, with all their friends in the church of Trull.

In 1573-4 there were three women churchwardens in Trull, Jone Bour (?), Jone Gensum and Ysbell Thomas. Their accounts show a credit balance at the end of the year. Joan Gensum died during her year of office. She was evidently a woman of means, for she was able to leave 'To Thomas Rowsewell, my son, £90. To Robert Cade, my son, £90', and after several other bequests the residue of her estate to her son John Cade. Her name is given as Joan Johnson of Trowle, Somerset, but she was certainly the same woman, as the death of Joan Jansum, widow, is in the burial register with the date 20th September 1574. Ysbell Thomas held office as one of the churchwardens again in 1575-6 and died the following year, leaving 6d for church expenses.

The churchwardens' accounts show that the same woman did the washing of church linen from 1572 until 1586. In the former year she is called Crysten Lanne and in the latter Christian Lambe; spelling was erratic in these old documents. She usually received 3d a year for her work, so the presumption is that the linen was not washed very often. (A labourer's wage at this time was about 8d a day.)

The name Joan appears to have been by far the most popular Christian name. In fact, there were so many in Trull that it must have created a certain amount of confusion.

11 Civil strife

We have a poignant reminder of how devastating the English Civil War must have been for people in Trull. The following is a transcript of a document in the parish archive:

'To the right honourable Sir John Stawell Knight of the Bath, Governor of Taunton present these

The humble petition of the Inhabitants of Trull desiring some reasonable allowance for the souldiers of Lieutenant Colonell Powells Company By those whose names are heerunto subscribed the xith of May 1644.

John Wood quartered Robert Sanders	5 weeks
Valentine Gardner quartered an ensigne & a Corporall	3 weeks
John Babb quartered Lieutenant Fugers & his horse	16 weeks
& his boy	4 weeks
William Buncombe quartered John Blake	4 weeks
Lucrese Keen widow quartered George Rosewell	5 weeks
Henry Wyatt quartered Copetone Granger	2 weeks
John Gill quartered Thomas Barklett	2 weeks
Willm Cogan quartered Roger Wolland	5 weeks
Robert Wood quartered Nathaniell Phillips & John Harris	5 weeks
Frauncis Cridland one more a souldier	4 daise
John Moore quartered Robert Edwards	1 week
Thomas Horte quartered George Tucker	5 weeks
Phillip Hayne quartered Robert Stevens	5 weeks
Anne Dight widow quartered William King	5 weeks
Willm Sherford quartered Richard Dare	5 weeks
John Baker quartered George Price	5 weeks
Xpofer (Christopher) Gardner quartered one souldier	1 week
William Dommett quartered Thomas Moore	1 week
George Durston quartered one Thomas Mo	3 weeks

Robert Wood	John Babb
Valentine Gardner	Henry Wyatt
Thomas Horte	Frances Credland
Lucrese Keene	William Sherford
William Cogan	Christopher Gardner
John Baker	William Domet
Phillip Hayne	John Moores
Ann Dight	George Durston
John Wood	John Gill'

Taunton and the surrounding villages had acquired a reputation as a centre of opposition to King Charles I, and a stronghold in which Puritan beliefs were free to flourish. In August 1642, when the Civil War between the forces of the king and Parliament finally broke out, Taunton was quick to declare itself for Parliament and at once became an island of resistance in a region generally loyal to the king. But in June 1643 a Royalist force captured the town and castle, and Sir John Stawell became its Governor.

Royalist soldiers were billeted on households in Taunton and the surrounding villages. We can only imagine the impact that hostile and sometimes rapacious soldiers had on the people they were billeted on, and the destitution they may have caused. We do not know if there was any response to the petition but that seems unlikely, particularly as only a few weeks later a Parliamentary force entered the town secretly, and within a few days the Royalist garrison had surrendered. The new Parliamentary governor was the famous Robert Blake.

The first of the Royalist sieges of Taunton began in October 1644, and, with one brief respite, lasted until May 1645. The besieging army grew to 6,000 men, and reports of the brutal indiscipline of the Royalist troops soon reached London. Villages were laid waste, repeated plundering, horrific rapes and local men were forced to hide to avoid summary hanging. The last glimpse we have of the impact on Trull is on 10th May, when the Parliamentary relief force of 7,000 men camped overnight in the fields of Pitminster, Poundisford and Trull. Then on the following day they relieved the siege, bringing 'unspeakable joy to the distressed inhabitants'. Two-thirds of the town was in ruins, many hundreds were dead, and in the ravaged countryside surrounding Taunton, presumably including Trull, the fields were as bare 'as if they had sowed salt'.

The Civil War effectively ended in 1651 following the execution of the king and the establishment of the Commonwealth led by Oliver Cromwell, who was declared to be Lord Protector. In Somerset, committees had been set up in 1646 to deal with clergy still loyal to the king.[1] Such men, called 'delinquents' or 'malignants', were removed from their parishes and replaced by 'ministers' of Puritan beliefs, a term used by the incumbents of Trull from 1623 to 1837. We know something of one of these, Benjamin Berry. He was incumbent here in July 1659. He had studied at Magdalen Hall, Oxford, and was a chorister in the college 1650-4. He married Elizabeth Polwheel at Whitchurch, Devon, in September 1655 and in 1656 was rector of Mary Tavy, Devon. He presumably moved to Trull a few years later.

In 1660, following the death of Oliver Cromwell and the failure of his son Richard, the monarchy was restored with King Charles II on the throne. But hundreds refused to accept the doctrines of the re-established Anglican Church, and flocked instead to nonconformist conventicles in local towns and villages including Trull. Charles had promised freedom of worship to all his subjects, but the Cavalier parliament would not let him honour that undertaking, being determined that everyone should attend Church of England services. The 1662 Act of Uniformity required all clergy to be, or have been, ordained by a bishop (abolished during the Commonwealth) and to use the *Book of Common Prayer* in its entirety. Some 1760 clergymen resigned their posts rather than conform, 62 of these being from Somerset parishes. The high number surely reflects the Puritan nature of Taunton and its environs.

One of these was Benjamin Berry. We subsequently hear of him 'preaching at Dulverton and in three other Somerset parishes' in 1669. He was licensed as of Exeter, 11th April 1672, also at Trull: application for license proposed as 'the places of Worshipp in the Parish Church of Trul (in the tyme of Vacancie) and the Church Howse of the said Parish … This is desired by the Generalitie of the parish' but was 'not granted'. So it looks as though he tried to return to minister in Trull but was refused. He afterwards lived at Topsham on the Exe estuary.[2]

King James II, a Roman Catholic, succeeded to the throne in 1685, and rumours of a planned rebellion began to fill the West Country. Then on 11th June, the Duke of Monmouth, King Charles II's favourite but illegitimate son, a Protestant, landed at Lyme Regis, and his ranks were swelling as they marched through Dorset and Somerset. On 18th June they reached Taunton, and Monmouth was greeted with wild enthusiasm. Twenty-seven 'maids of Taunton' presented him with flags for his troops, and at the market cross he was proclaimed King. But on 6th July he was decisively defeated at the battle of Sedgemoor.

Retribution was swift. Monmouth was executed in London on 15th July. By this time, Colonel Kirke, with his Tangier regiment, had reached Taunton, and had 19 of the rebels hanged, drawn and quartered. Then on 18th September, Judge Jeffreys opened the Bloody Assizes in the great hall of Taunton Castle, with 514 prisoners on trial. Of these, 144 were condemned to hang, and 284 sentenced to transportation.

We know the fate of some of these from Trull. George Gaylard was a highly respected yeoman who lived with his wife Meller and family in a farmhouse at Brown's Elm, at the top of Amberd Lane. He served as churchwarden, as tithingman, and carried a sword in the militia. But he joined the rebels, and was hanged at Stogumber.

In Evelyn Solway's fascinating autobiography[3] she had researched her family members at that time. John Moggridge of Pitminster, a serge weaver with a family of wife and five children, was convicted of 'taking up arms against the King' and was hanged at Weston Zoyland. His son John was also convicted but was transported to Barbados, where he was sold into slavery. His other son William was pardoned. Two other relatives were killed in the Battle of Sedgemoor.

In a petition for relief to the Bishop of Winchester, in 1692, Sarah Edwards of Trull describes how her late husband John 'being unhappily concerned in Monmouth's Rebellion was convicted thereof, and thereupon banished into Virginia and is since dead in Mary Land'. She had been left with six children to support and was heavily in debt.[4]

Much of the above is gleaned from Tom Mayberry's graphic and comprehensive account of the events of the Civil War and Monmouth Rebellion in the Vale of Taunton.[5]

References
1. RW Dunning, *Christianity in Somerset*, Somerset County Council (1976).
2. AG Matthews, *Calamy Revised, being a revision of Edmund Calamy's Account of the Ministers and Others Ejected and Silenced 1660-2*, Oxford University Press (1934).
3. E Solway, *A Trull Girl's Story*, published privately, 2011.
4. SHC, DD/SP 22/9 petition, transcribed by Adrian Webb.
5. T Mayberry, *The Vale of Taunton Past*, Phillimore & Co (1998).

12 The care of the poor

'Overseers of the Poor' were responsible for administering the Poor Laws passed during the last few years of the reign of Queen Elizabeth I. In Trull three substantial householders served as overseers each year. Their work was a heavy burden, and until 1800 they received no payment unless they undertook the post out of their turn. They collected rates from each of the three tithings and submitted their accounts to the parishioners at Easter each year.

Clothing, blankets and sometimes wood were bought for the poor, and the entry 'gave a Croker towards a fiddle 15s' is an unusual one. Help 'towards a burial' was given, and in 1709 the overseers paid 'for wool about several persons putting into their coffins 3s 10d'. Acts of 1666 and 1678 had made it compulsory for everyone to be buried in woollen stuff, and the Burial Register in the church gives many pages of entries to which certificates of burial in woollen are added.

Occupiers of certain holdings were obliged to take poor children as apprentices, whom they had to keep, thereby saving the parish expense and ensuring that the child was not likely to become a charge on the rates when he or she grew up. In 1675 a dispute between the parishioners of Trull and Thomas Vilven was settled at Quarter Sessions, the order being 'that the parishioners shall pay Thomas 20s towards providing clothes for Francis Stroud, an apprentice placed on him in respect of an estate in the said parish which he rents from Edward Babb and that thereupon Stroud shall remain with him as his apprentice'. At the same time Edward Thomas was ordered to keep Justine Stroud as an apprentice.

Children were bound as apprentices when they were eight or nine years old, and for nearly all of them in Trull their trade was 'the art and science of husbandry' or the 'art and mystery of housewifery'.

Fitzroy Jones[1] wrote: 'Settlement was the term used to describe the belonging of a person to a parish with the right to maintenance should need arise'. The following removal order shows how anxious a parish was not to be burdened with poor people legally settled elsewhere:

'Whereas complaint hath been made unto us two of His Majesty's Justices of the Peace by you the churchwardens and overseers of the Poor in the parish of Worle in the County of Somerset that Thomas Cottle, Edith his wife, Elizabeth and Mary their children have lately intruded themselves into the said parish of Worle there to inhabit as Parishioners contrary to the Laws relating to settlement of the Poor and are there likely to become chargeable and that they have no ways gained a legal settlement in the said parish of Worle but that their last legal place of settlement is in the parish of Trill otherwise Trull in the County of Somerset. These are therefore in His Majesty's name to order and require you the churchwardens and overseers of the Poor of the parish of Trill otherwise Trull that you or some of you do remove and convey the said Thomas Cottle, Edith his wife, Elizabeth and Mary their children into the parish of Trill otherwise Trull and there provide for them as their own parishioners. Given under our hand and seal this fourteenth day of April 1738. Thomas Prowse, John Selwood'.

An illegitimate child was a source of concern to the overseers as it was liable to become a charge on the parish. For some years from 1636 it cost 1s 8d a week to keep such a child. If the father could be shown to belong to another parish, the mother and child were removed there as soon as possible.

The churchwardens often paid items which should really have been paid by the overseers, and vice versa. In the extract from the churchwardens' accounts of 1702-3 (see page 53), the money paid to the constable 'for carrying vagrants thorow the County' should have been the responsibility of the overseers; but they, on the other hand, occasionally paid for bread and wine for communion. Examples such as these show the close connection between church and civil administration up to the 18th century, strengthened in Trull by the practice, which was by no means general, of the churchwardens for one year becoming two of the overseers for the following year.

As well as the regular 'Poor List', there were other persons known as the Second Poor, who could normally support themselves but who needed occasional assistance when they were ill. Assistance in childbirth was very infrequently given until 1770, but after that payments were often made either to the midwife or to the expectant mother, or to both. Betty Ridwood served as a midwife from 1795 to 1812. The poor got medical attention at the expense of the parish, but until 1674 women were paid for cures and healing. After that date the poor were generally attended by a doctor, and from 1785 a regular parish doctor received an annual fee of 4 guineas, which was increased to 5 guineas in 1797. Small pox was a scourge in the 18th century, but the first records of inoculation in Trull are followed by entries of payment for coffins for two of the inoculated children. So it is hardly surprising that there are no further records of inoculation until 1808.

In July 1621 at the Taunton Quarter Sessions a petition was made 'from the churchwardens of Trull, together with the overseers and sydemen and diverse other inhabitants, to be allowed to erect two cottages for the use of the poor of the parish upon some waste ground of the Lord of the manor … who hath given his consent'. The following April at the Ilchester Sessions a committee of three men was appointed to enquire into the truth of a counter petition 'by the most sufficientest men of Trull against the building of two cottages there for the poor, in that there are enough cottages there already and that the site is unfitting …'. In the meantime the cottages were 'to be stayed'. The next January at Wells this committee reported that they 'find that all the doubts, objections and grievances do proceed more out of a wilful and forward disposition than any just cause of complaint; and that in their opinion it is a necessary work, there being a great number of poor people there, and the place very fitting'. As a result of this report an order was made allowing the cottages to be built.

The overseers' accounts before 1624 are not preserved, and Fitzroy Jones, in his article,[1] makes no mention of these Poor Houses. Doubtless they housed some of the regular poor, each of whom, after 1697, would have worn on his right shoulder a large 'P' for 'Pauper' followed by 'T' for 'Trull' in red or blue cloth. The two cottages were demolished in 1904, three years after this drawing was made, in order to enlarge the churchyard.

In 1802 and 1810 three properties belonging to the parish were sold, and the money raised was used to build four brick Poor Houses at the top of Mill Lane, adjoining the churchyard. Subsequently the Poor Law of 1834 grouped parishes into 'Unions' and paupers, aged, sick or able-bodied, were sent (children with their parents) to the unpopular Union Workhouse in Trinity Road, Taunton.

The four cottages were eventually made into two. This drawing was made for the first edition of this book in 1953. The cottages were finally demolished in the 1960s to make way for the present garages at the top of Mill Lane.

The concept of meeting the housing needs of local people with low incomes has continued to this day. Beginning with the 1919 Housing Act, local authorities were empowered to provide council houses. These could be general housing for the working class, general housing, part of slum clearance programmes or just homes provided for the most needy. They could be funded directly by local councils, through central government incentive or by revenue obtained when other houses were sold.

THE POOR-HOUSES OF 1810

Taunton Rural District Council bought Upper Hoges from the Wyatt Charity (see page 95) after WWII as the site for 24 new Council houses, to be called 'Wyatts Field'. Other post-war Council housing in Trull included Brookside Close, Trull Green and the north side of Mill Lane. Since the 1980 Housing Act brought in the 'Right to Buy', many of these have been purchased by their tenants at a very generous discount, and subsequent extensions and modifications have made the developments unrecognisable as former council houses.

In recent years, government and local authority policy has encouraged the provision of 'affordable' housing, to rent or purchase at a discount – typically 70% of the normal market value. Planning permission can be granted 'in exceptional circumstances' for a development on agricultural land which would not otherwise be allowed. The developer can therefore purchase the land at its agricultural value, allowing the properties to be bought or rented for an 'affordable' sum to people with both local connections and low income.

In 2007 Trull Parish Council commissioned a survey of housing needs in the parish.[2] It concluded that '18 households or individuals are currently unable to buy or rent on the open market and therefore require housing which both suits their needs and is affordable in order to allow them to remain living and in some cases working in the Parish'. Taunton Deane Borough Council accepted this evidence of need, and eventually granted planning permission for Dipford Orchard (below), a development of 9 – subsequently 11 – affordable houses, 4 for rental through a local housing association and the rest for purchase, by applicants with local connections and low incomes.

Taunton Deane BC's Local Plan required developers to include a proportion of affordable housing in any new development. As a result, both Gatchell Oaks in 2007 and Amingford Mead in 2016 included affordable houses alongside other full-priced ones.

References
1. F Jones, 'Some Aspects of Poor Law Administration, Seventeenth to Nineteenth Centuries, from Trull Overseers' Accounts' in *Proceedings of the Somerset Archaeological Society*, XCV (1950).
2. Community Council for Somerset, *Trull Parish Housing Needs Report* (2007).

13   Trull Charities

Trull Parish Lands Community Fund
The Trull Parish Lands Community Fund's origin is in a pre-Reformation religious guild or lay fraternity, dedicated to the Virgin Mary and known as 'the service of Our Lady of Trull'. All such chantries were dissolved by an Act passed in 1547 at the beginning of Edward VI's reign, during which a more Protestant version of the Reformation took place. The following year a survey was made of all property belonging to Chantries, Fraternities, Guilds etc. It was recorded under the heading 'Trulle. The service of our lady ther' that 'There is a ten[emen]t in Pytmyster … the yelding whereof John Forde of Pytmyster sold unto William Voysey of Trulle for £12.1.0 sterling and after the decease of the foresaide John fforde, the saide William solde the yelding of the saide ten[emen]t to the s[er]vice of oure lady in Trull, ther to remayne'. 'The store', i.e. fund or property, of Our Lady of Trull came to be administered by the churchwardens, and subsequently by the Trull Parish Lands Charity.

A decree of 1609 states that 'from time immemorial there had been divers copyhold lands, tenements and cottages, parcel of the Manor of Taunton and Taunton Dean, belonging to and for the use of the said Parish of Trull, as well for the relief of the poor there and repairing of the church, as also for setting forth of soldiers and placing of poor children within the said parish'. These lands had been surrendered to John and William Smith as tenants without any written agreement and although they had paid rent during the first three or four years of their tenancy, they had since refused to do so, and had 'made a private profit of those things which should have been for the public good of the said parish'. The Smiths were ordered to surrender the lands to the lord of the manor and to hold them according to the custom of the manor, employing the whole profit for the charitable purposes mentioned above.

Throughout the 18th century and for most of the 19th century the rents of parish lands were entered in the churchwardens' account books. These accounts are missing for almost the whole of the 17th century, but in an Elizabethan account book, dating from 1571, there is an entry in 1582 'Item payd to John Smyth of Galmington for the discharging of the shriffes booke for Rixam 2s 2d'. The same year the entry 'Item received of William Palmer for the rent of Rixam for one year' has been deleted, and in 1587 an item concerning the lord's rent at Half Yard has also been deleted. In 1573 'Item payd to the settying furthe of soldyers 20s', various sums paid to poor people between 1571 and 1588, and the large expenditure on the church fabric between 1585 and 1589, may have been made from funds received for rent of parish land, not from William Palmer's private benefaction as was conjectured in chapter 8. The deletion of entries points to the probability that the churchwardens kept a separate account book for the funds of the charity and sometimes entered items in the wrong book by mistake.

There were frequent complaints of the misuse of charitable funds in the 17th century. For instance in 1688 John Baker issued a bill of complaint against Harry Bayley (the minister) and John Crosse, John Thomas and William Owsley; and in 1696 Richard, Bishop of Bath and Wells, and three others were Commissioners for an enquiry following a complaint that the funds of the charity had been 'misgoverned, misemployed and misconverted'. They wrote 'To the present Churchwardens and Overseers for six years last past or to as many of them as are now living', directing them to attend a court of enquiry at Wells.

Lands formerly belonging to Trull Parish Lands Charity were:

- Rixam (or Rixham or Ricksome) Mead, consisting of one and a half acres in the parish of Bishops Hull. The wardens of Our Lady's store acquired it in 1542-3, and it was still held by Trull parish in 1838-9, when Colonel Pearson was the tenant paying £5 rent. There appears to be no further mention of Rixam in the churchwardens' accounts, but the receipt of £2 12s 6d for timber thrown on Stepswater Meadow in 1859-60 must refer to Rixam, which was in the district known as Stepswater, now a built-up area on the Wellington Road. This property was later known as Trull Acre, and was sold by the trustees of the charity in 1910.
- Yard, or Half Yard, was the place where most of the timber was felled for the work done in the church in 1587-8. It was in the parish of Pitminster and was probably near Barton Grange, as far as can be ascertained from the Pitminster tithe apportionment of 1838. The wardens of Our Lady's store held it in the early 16th century. The churchwardens of Trull received £2 10s rent for it in 1736-7, but by 1744-5 the rent for Half Yard was coupled with that of 'Louton' at £21.
- Lowton is also in Pitminster, but it has not been possible to determine the exact position of the 20 acres there owned by the charity at least from 1702. This property was exchanged in 1803 or 1804 with Mr Thomas Southwood for about the same acreage of land known as Totterdells Farm, on the road from Taunton to Cheddon Fitzpaine, and this was not sold until 1913.
- A house in East Reach, Taunton, known as 'Trull Lands', was held by the charity as early as 1702-3. It was sold in 1810 to Mr Wyatt for £125. In the early 16th century the wardens of Our Lady's store had a house in Taunton referred to as 'Our Lady's house'. This may be the origin of the house in East Reach.

All the other lands held by the charity were in the parish of Trull:

- One of these was 'a piece of ground consisting of about a quarter of an acre lying in Trull Green, formerly the site of a house which used to be let at 5s a year'. This was almost certainly occupied by John Stephens in 1842 and owned by Sarah Stephens, for the Charity Report states that it was sold to Mr Stevens in 1802 for £10. The former house on this site was bringing in £3 a year rent between 1732 and 1744, the earlier year marking the earliest reference found anywhere to Trull Green. It seems likely that Trull Green was formerly known as Cockshayes Green: for in 1647 the survey of the Manor of Taunton Deane (North Trendle Tithing) shows that Thomas Knight held one cottage in Cockshayes Green for which he paid 4d lord's rent; and in 1744-5 the churchwardens paid 6d lord's rent for Knight House. Again in 1801-2, just before its sale, the Churchwardens received 5s rent for Knight Garden. The name Cockshaye can be identified with the Cockage of 1207-8 on page 11.

- The other property sold in 1802 was Cob Garden, also about a quarter of an acre, on the road to Angersleigh. This is now known as Stone House, having been rebuilt in stone during the last century. The churchwardens received 5s rent for it in 1801-2, and it was sold the following year to Mr Southwood for £10. It had probably been held by the parish at least since the middle of the 17th century; for the survey of 1647 for Woodland Tithing states that the wardens of Trull paid 2d lord's rent for one cottage belonging to the parish, and there is no evidence that any other property was ever held by them which could have been in this tithing.

The money raised by the sale of these three properties was used to build the poor houses adjoining the churchyard. But the *Charity Report* of 1821 states that the rents of land still in the hands of the parish were carried to the churchwardens' general account and were not applied towards the relief of the poor. The accounts for 1809-10 show that £115 19s 1d was spent on brick and tile, so that it was evidently in this year that the last poor houses were built (see page 65). When the Poor Law Unions began to house the poor, the former poor houses were let, and it is clear from the tithe apportionment that there were four brick cottages and that they adjoined the poor house of 1622. The latter was pulled down in 1904 when the churchyard was enlarged, and the brick cottages remained in the possession of the trustees of the charity until they were sold in 1952.

The *Charity Report* of 1821 states that the parish had five acres of arable land lying in the middle of Batt's estate, and this is marked 'Parish Field' in the tithe map. Though it is some distance from Batts House (later Batts Park) it is evidently in the area known as Batts; for the Pitminster tithe apportionment shows that the farm called Haygrove, where the old mill is situated, was called Batts in 1838-9. This field can be identified with the parish property formerly known as Lady Liscombe from the fact that other fields nearby are Great Liscombe and Liscombe Mead. The churchwardens' accounts for 1713-14 show that James Tucker was paying £3 10s rent for Liscombe in 1713-14. In 1744-5 the widow Coles paid £8 rent for 'Ladyland and Lady Liscombe and the Churchyard'. The Parish Close (Lady Liscombe) was sold for £500 in 1884, not long before the agricultural depression set in. In the early 16th

century the wardens of Our Lady's store held some land called 'Luscombe'. This must be the origin of Liscombe/Lady Liscombe/ Parish Field referred to in later documents.

Ladyland or Lady Land adjoined the churchyard and part of it was taken to enlarge the latter in 1904. Another part bordering on Wild Oak Lane was sold in 1950, but the greater part of the meadow was sold in 1987 for a housing development called Ladylawn, the cul-de-sac beside Chantry Cottage. Ladyland and Lady Liscombe must have been held by the Charity at least since 1647, when the survey of the Manor of Taunton Deane includes the payment of 16s 2½d lord's rent by the parishioners of Trull for 'One cottage and certain overland' in North Trendle Tithing.

In 1873 the Charity Commissioners issued a 'Scheme for the Management and Regulation' of the 'Church or Parish Lands Charity in the parish of Trull'. The trustees were to be the vicar and churchwardens ex officio and seven other 'respectable persons'. The first non-official trustees were Henry Jefferies Badcock, banker, Trull; Benjamin Denning, gentleman, Comeytrowe, Trull; Richard Greenslade, auctioneer, Trull; Thomas Burnaford Harness, MD Southwick House (now King's Gatchell), Trull; Henry Sweep, solicitor, Trull; Reverend William Jefferys Allen, of Gatchell House, Trull; and Thomas Blake, gentleman, Cutsey, Trull.

At this date the charity still owned Lady Liscombe (the Parish Field), Rixham mead and Totterdells as well as Ladyland and the former poor houses. The trustees were directed to apply a quarter of the net annual income of the Charity towards the maintenance and repair of the fabric of the parish church; a quarter towards the school; and the remaining half at their discretion to the relief of distress arising from sickness or other causes, to provident societies and for helping the 'poor inhabitants' in a variety of ways.

The funds of the charity are still administered according to these directions, which were incorporated when the Scheme was revised in 1994. The trustees are the rector of Trull and Headteacher of Trull School ex officio; a nominee of Trull Parish Council, Comeytrowe Parish Council (now part of Taunton Parish), and All Saints PCC; and three co-opted trustees. Those eligible for 'relief in need' are the parishioners of Trull and those parts of Comeytrowe in Trull parish until the boundary change in 1983 (see page 6). In the financial year 2018/19 the income was £22,000, of which £16,000 was spent. The shortfall reflects the difficulty in identifying people in need within the area covered by the Trust who are willing to apply for 'charity'. As a result, the name was officially changed to Community Fund in 2020.

John Buncombe's Stocking Charity
John Buncombe's Stocking Charity was founded in 1785. In his will, he 'Gave 50 Pounds to ye Augmentation of this Living also he Gave 20 Shillings a year to buy Stockings for the poor Children that goes to Mr Wyatts Charity School (see page 95) to be Paid out of his Lands in

Trull Moor' (as you can see on the charity board on the wall at the west end of the south aisle of the parish church). It was used particularly for school-leavers, so they were adequately dressed for agricultural or service employment. It continued to distribute hosiery to children of Trull School in special need until 1957, and in 1966 its capital of some £50 was incorporated into the Parish Lands Charity, with the consent of the Charity Commission.

The Marke and Norman Charities
In 1904 Theophilus Tripe Marke left a sum of money for the nursing of the sick poor and the benefit, at the discretion of the minister and churchwardens, of the deserving poor of Trull parish. In 1906 Miss Caroline Norman (who also paid for the church clock) made a bequest towards the payment and maintenance of a district nurse for the benefit of the sick. These two charities are now administered together. In 2018 their income was £171, of which £22 was spent. The previous year £628 was spent, after several years in which the income had been allowed to accumulate. The churchwardens remain the trustees.

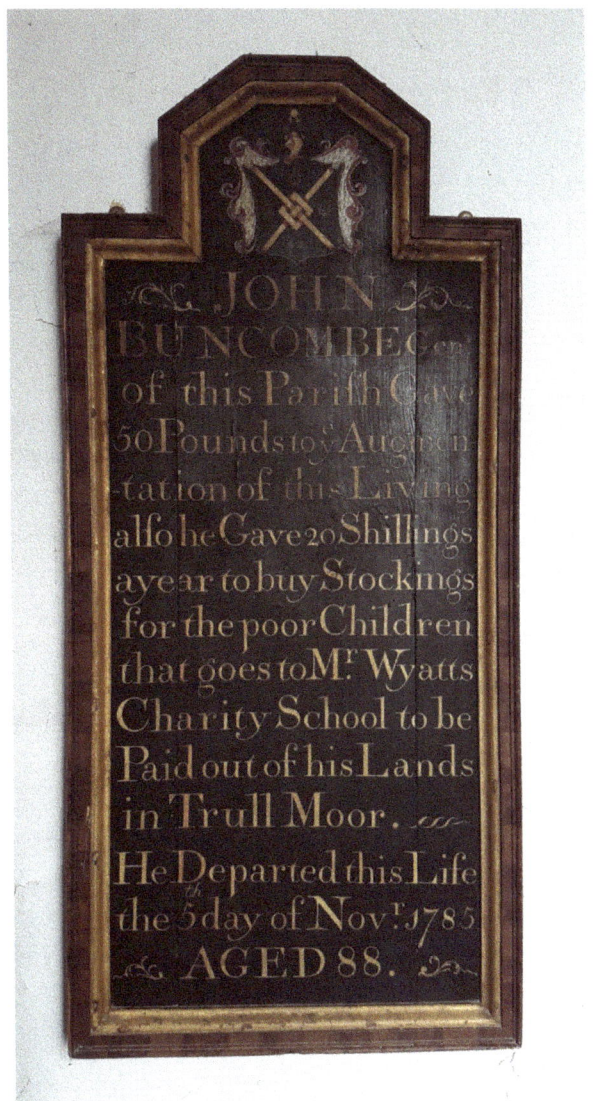

14 The Farms of Trull

Introduction

It has been impossible to investigate the history of every farm in the parish. A selection has been made, which includes the most significant ones. A brief account of the later history of the Manor of Taunton Deane will help to explain some of the terms used in the accounts of the farms.

In 1647 the manor was sequestered from the Bishop of Winchester and sold to Roger Hill, but it was restored to the see of Winchester in 1660. A survey made by an ordinance of Parliament before the sale in 1647 gives a complete list of all the holdings in the manor. These are of two sorts, one called Bondland, 'which have been and commonly are ancient dwelling tenements; the other called Overland, whereupon in ancient time there were no dwellings'. Bondland was held 'by a customary fine and rent certain, paying heriots (the best beast to the lord on the death of the holder), and doing other suits and services to the same belonging'. But those who held overland did not have to pay heriot or do any service for their land.

In the 1647 survey John Cox held two cottages in North Trendle tithing, for which the annual rent was 1s 7½d. and 'two Daynes rent'. This is the only record that in 1647 service to the lord of the manor was still liable to be enforced in Trull. The measures of land in 1647 do not seem to bear any definite relation to the lord's rent paid for them. As far as can be ascertained, a yardland was about 30 acres and a farthing about 7½ acres, but the holdings probably originated as strips of a given width but of varying lengths. The name 'Farthings' still belongs to a small farm in the parish. The ending 'hay' in so many of the place names is derived from the Anglo-Saxon 'hege' (hedge).

In 1822 the Manor of Taunton Deane was sold by the See of Winchester to Thomas Southwood of Leigh House, Angersleigh. He left it to his steward Reuben Mattock, whose nephew Robert Mattock was still lord of the manor in 1866. It seems probable that all or most of the farmhouses were built of cob or wood before the 16th century. There is no stone in the parish suitable for building, and the cost of transporting stone would have been heavy.

Budleigh

Richard of Buddlegh contributed 1s to the King's Exchequer in 1327-8. The parish registers show that there were three families living at Budley in the first half of the 16th century, their names being Heryng, Domet and Thomas. Budleigh Farm and Budleigh are two separate farms now, and were so in 1842. The curious way in which the land is divided between them supports the story that a former owner left his land to his two daughters. The fields on the east of the lane from Budleigh to Steart are in alternate ownership. There have been practically no changes in field boundaries in the last hundred years, but the three copses were orchards in 1842.

In 1965 the Comeytrowe and District Women's Institute produced a scrap book to commemorate the Golden Jubilee year of the National Federation of Women's Institutes. One of the contributors was CH Corder who, with her husband Alan, was farming Budleigh at that time. Entitled 'Down on the farm 1965', readers were informed that there were 41 Ayrshire cows and heifers on 55 acres. With the exception of a fortnight these were kept out all winter. The spring was cold but dry, which allowed them to make good progress with the spring cultivations. The second half of June was very wet which wrecked their 3,000 bales of hay, but the apple harvest was good. As for the future, the Corders had decided that they would have to change to milking Friesians. With milk prices lower than ten years ago, Jerseys or Friesians were their only option. Mrs Corder ends her account of the farming year: 'We wonder what will be the future of the small dairy farmer'. The answer was Alan and Heather Corder did change to Friesians, and continued milking for another 24 years. The herd was dispersed in 1989 and the Corders sold up two years later. They had been at Budleigh since 1956 and had five children, so when the house needed rethatching, for safety's sake, they opted to have the roof tiled.

When the Corders moved in, the other Budleigh farm was already occupied by Victor deGex, and when he sold up he built himself a bungalow the other side of the road. The Corders' house was bought by Tim Everett, an art restorer, who lived there until quite recently. Budleigh House Farm has been farmed by Mark and Sue Steele who since 2006 have been breeding

Alpacas. The rest of the land that previously made up these two farms is now owned and farmed by Andrew Burrough, who lives in the barn conversion on the opposite side of the road from the two farmhouses. Andrew and his father moved here from Fullards Farm where they had also been renting Canonsgrove Farm.

In 1974 EHD Williams, who was a considerable authority on Somerset vernacular buildings, recorded that Budleigh Farmhouse had a 2-room and cross-passage plan, plus lean-to, and jointed-cruck roof timbers, windows with ovolo mouldings, and a bacon-curing chamber alongside the S fireplace. The house was interpreted as originating in the 16th century but extended north in the 17th century and the lean-to added. It has window mullions and framings of Ham stone. The steeply pitched roof was thatched. The date 1653 is on a fire-back in an open chimney piece, though this, of course, might be a later importation. The house belonging to Budleigh, the other farm, was built in the 19th century, and is said to have replaced one that was burnt down.

Castleman's Hill

Situated on the site of a Hill Fort, very little is known of the history of this farm, but several legends are associated with it. According to FW Matthews, in *Tales of the Blackdown Borderland* (1923): 'A dragon is said to have haunted the district, and levied a toll of human life, till at last he was met and slain by a valiant knight, and the field where the monster drew his last breath was furrowed up by the lashing of his tail, and the hollow remains in the field to this day'. Formerly 'a dragon was a werme, and Wormstall is the name of the field'. In Home Field is the head of a short valley, and the furrows are obvious, but neither this nor any other field on this farm or in the parish bears the name of Wormstall, nor was there such a name in the tithe apportionment of 1842. Mr Vivian Neal has suggested that the dragon story may originally have been derived from the memory of a Saxon raid, as the dragon-standard was the symbol of 'Saxon Kingship'. He has also pointed out the possibility that the choice of subjects for the 'Dragon' window in Trull church (see page 41) may have been inspired by the legend of the Castleman's Hill dragon.

Part of the farmhouse is probably medieval. It is built of grey Triassic stone from a quarry at Rumwell and of Lias limestone. The fine brick chimney-stacks, now demolished, were 17th century. In the 19th century most of the panelling from the house was taken away and put in Rumwell Hall, but the oak staircase remains.

The story persisted that the Duke of Monmouth during his ill-fated rebellion had stayed at Castleman's Hill. Apparently in the 1860s the tenants there grew so tired of being pestered by visitors asking to see the bed in which Monmouth was supposed to have slept that eventually they burnt it - and were turned out of the farm by their landlord as a result. Another story for which no confirmation has been found is that Castleman's Hill was the headquarters of the Royalists at the siege of Taunton during the Civil War.

In 1635 John Crosse of Castleman's Hill was allotted two seats in Trull church, but no other reference to the farm has been found among the parish documents before the 19th century. Stone from Rumwell quarry is said to have been carried by donkeys up the old cart track to Trull church. Mr Thomas Bevis, who lived at Castleman's Hill at the end of the 19th century, later remembered that the farm was mainly grass then, but was told that it had formerly been largely arable. He kept a hundred pigs when he was there. The employment of small children as bird scarers at 2d a day had only recently gone out at that time.

In the 1960s and early 1970s Castleman's Hill was farmed by the Watts family. They milked a herd of Friesians and for a while this milk was sent to Hamwood to be made into cheese. When in 1976 the farm was sold Cyril Webber, who was farming Herswell, became the new owner. He then moved in to Castleman's Hill where he believed there to have been a tunnel to the house at Rumwell Manor but after much searching no sign of it was ever found. It was Cyril Webber who constructed the new driveway that went from Herswell through Castleman's Hill and on to the A38 at Rumwell. This changed the orientation of the farm away from Trull towards Rumwell, and when the Venn family of Newley Farm, Bishops Hull, bought it in 1986 this situation became even more apparent. At the time of the sale Castleman's Hill Farm was 176 acres and was described in the sale particulars as 'The well situated and productive dairy/arable farm (and including an established farmhouse cider business)'. Included in the sale were various items of cider making equipment, together with approximately 10,000 gallons of unconsumed farmhouse cider. Following the sale Castleman's Hill became part of the Venn family's other holdings which by the early 2010s totalled 1,300 acres and also included four fields previously part of George's Farm. For 20 years the Farmhouse was let as a hostel for teenagers but currently Dennis Venn's grandson, William, and his wife are living there.

Chilliswood

In 1327-8, the first year of the reign of Edward III, the occupier of Chilliswood must have been the richest man in Trendle, for it is recorded that, from Dupeforde (Dipford) Tithing, Nicholas of Chiliwordiswode paid 2s tax to the Exchequer, 4d more than that paid by anyone else in the parish. Henry Wood of Culmstock, Devon, whose will was proved in November 1627, left 'Lands called Chillenwood, in Trull, to my son Robert Wood, and if he die then to my sons John and Edward'. Robert evidently inherited the land, for in the church seating plan of 1635 Mr Robert Wood held four seats, one 'pro Davidge of Chillerswood', another 'pro Davidge', another 'pro Daws', and another 'pro Pulmans'. The same year the overseers of the poor paid 2s 11d for a smock for Mr Wood's apprentice. In 1644 he quartered two soldiers of the Royalist forces for five weeks. In 1647 Robert Wood held 'Three Messuages and half a yard and one Five Acre of Bondland with certain Overland', for which he paid £2 6s 2¼d lord's rent, more than anyone else in the parish. In 1664-5 Robert Wood paid 12s in hearth tax for the six hearths he owned. Since these were in three separate houses, the farmhouse at Chilliswood must have been comparatively small at that time. The rental of Hull and Holway Hundreds for 1744-5 shows that John Dymond paid £2 7s 5¾d lord's rent for Chilliswood. John Dymond was one of the overseers of the poor in 1748, and, from the special certificate attached to the accounts for this year, it appears that he was a Quaker and therefore made an affirmation instead of taking the oath before one of His Majesty's Justices of the Peace.

In 1812 Chilliswood was bought by another Quaker, James Hewett, who purchased the neighbouring holdings of Rackhouse and Coxe's three years later. Every Sunday he drove to the Friends' Meeting House in Taunton, and the people of Trull said they 'could always tell the time by Mr Hewett going by in his carriage'. He had 15 children, three of whom died in infancy. Mary, his eldest daughter, was converted by William Mason, an itinerant Bible Christian, who preached at Daw's Green Cottage. When she was 21 she defied her stern father, left home to become a travelling preacher herself, and afterwards married William Mason. The Hewetts had moved to Burlescombe and Commander James Vibart, RN, was owner of Chilliswood in 1842 and was still there in 1861. Dr. Purvis lived in the house in the 1930s and experimented in the fields with a huge wheel called a Dynasphere, which had a motor inside it, and seats in which passengers could sit while the wheel revolved round them. The Douglas Motor Company took some interest in this machine but it never became a commercial proposition.

Chilliswood has changed hands many times since then, and was farmed with Hamwood for some years. In 1950 the Hawkings brothers sold Chilliswood Farm to Frank and Margaret Henson. When Taunton was severely flooded on the 27th October 1960 their son Graham was photographed in Station Road ferrying stranded inhabitants to their place of work. Permission to use this photograph was granted by the Somerset County Gazette.

The complex and much-altered house occupies the south and east sides of a courtyard, with a converted barn on the north. The east range of the house, which may have included a medieval hall, contains a lateral stack, jointed-cruck roof trusses, mullioned windows, and a smoke chamber at the N end. The south range, which seems to have been added in the 16th century, contains stud-and-panel partitions and a winding-stair, but the S front was remodelled in Tudor style in 1835 and has a reset plaque dated 1594 together with a W initial (for Wood?). The former barn has jointed crucks and a later polygonal horse-engine house on the north side (now a separate dwelling). An infill between the east end of the barn and the east range of the house includes 17th century moulded ceiling beams on the ground floor and some external timber-framing on the first floor. In recent years the house has been comprehensively restored by the Hensons' daughter Anne and her husband.

Canonsgrove Farm

Until the 20th century there were two farms at Canonsgrove, Upper and Lower. In the *Register of Electors* for 1832 Samuel Osborne was occupying 100 acres of land at Lower Canonsgrove and Poundisford. He and his wife Dinah née Trood, daughter of John Trood of Spearcey Farm, had married in 1827. But in October 1838 he and their five year old daughter, Elizabeth, contracted Scarlet Fever and both died. Hence on the 1841 census Dinah is shown farming Canonsgrove on her own, as well as bringing up her three daughters, Dinah, Mary and Jane. By 1851 Dinah had relinquished the tenancy and moved out. Reuben Mattock was the next tenant, and Lower Canonsgrove was still a separate farm when in 1908 a Mr Hall quit the tenancy, holding his dispersal sale on 23rd April.

Higher Canonsgrove at the time of the tithe apportionment was both owned and farmed by John Hine. When he retired John Hine jnr. carried on farming the 110 acres, but when he left the farm was let to Isaac Bicknell who was occupying the farm in 1871. Also living at Canonsgrove Farm at that time was William George Cann, known as George. From the Cann Family History we are told that George never went to school, apparently he refused to! Instead, from the age of six or seven, he worked at Canonsgrove Farm, a mile or so from his family's cottage. At the farm, he lived over the pigsty. An old man at the farm who worked with him had asthma and George had great fun imitating his wheezing. Eventually the old man died and George was one of the coffin bearers. A few nights later, George was in bed asleep above the pigsty when he was woken by the sound of the old man's breathing! He thought he had come back to haunt him. Shaking with fright, he got up, but could see nothing. Creeping down the ladder to the pigsty, he heard the noise again. It was one of the pigs! George later moved to Eastbrook working for a farrier before moving on again to Puriton, where he worked as a blacksmith. George died in Bridgwater in 1950 age 92.

Canonsgrove remained in the Hine family until September 1924 when the three farms belonging to the estate of the late Miss Susan Hine were auctioned. Lot 2 was Canonsgrove Farm with a house containing some fine old oak panelling, extensive outbuildings and 58½ acres of meadow, orchard and arable land let at £120 per annum to Mr WH Avery. Starting at £2,000 bidding reached £2,600 at which figure Mr FH Palmer of Yarcombe became the purchaser. Mr Avery relinquished the tenancy the following year and the Palmers moved in. Six years later the neighbouring farm, Fullards, came on the market and Mr Palmer bought that one as well. By the end of the war the farm had passed to their son, Basil. He became famous or possibly infamous for the production of Basil Palmer's farmhouse cider.

When Basil died in 1971, the Burroughs family who had been farming Fullards then farmed both farms and Mrs Palmer stayed in Canonsgrove farmhouse. In 1974 the two farms became separated by the motorway, and when Mrs Palmer died in 1997 the farms passed to her nephew, Colin Ralph. The combined size at that time was 105 acres. Like Peter Parris of Kibbear and Sidney French of Spearcey, Colin devoted much of his time to serving on Trull Parish Council, including much practical voluntary work.

Cutsey
In 1327 there was paid to the Exchequer of King Edward III 'De Henrico de Cuttleshegh 12s 1d' and 'De Joanne de Cuttleshegh 10d'. In the church seating plan of 1635 there was a seat for John Babb of Cutsey and another for his wife. Steart was a separate holding at this time, for Mr James Cade's wife is described as 'of Stiert'. Cutsey had come into the hands of the Blake family by 1700, when Mr Robert Blake paid 13s 8d lord's rent for Cutsey, £1 for Harpers and 9s for land 'late Priests', while the same year Mr Thomas Gatchell paid 12s 9d for 'Start'. Forty four years later Mr Richard Black (Blake) of 'Cutshay' was paying the same

lord's rent for Cutsey and Harpers, 2s for land called 'Thomas', 2s for 'Pococks', 9s for 'his brother Thomas' and 4d for 'late John Sayers', so that the Blake family increased their holdings considerably in the first half of the 18th century. Steart was still a separate farm, for which Mrs Gatchell paid 12s 9d in 1744-5.

The land belonging to Cutshay in 1842 included Steart and Reaphay. The road from Harpers to West Buckland passed close to Cutsey House on the west side of it, instead of some distance to the east as it does at present. One of the fields was a detached part of Angersleigh Parish. Cutsey Covert had not been planted. The small holding of Lipe Hill was owned by William Blake and occupied by Mary Amery. There have been a large number of changes in the field boundaries since 1842. William Blake, who owned the farm in 1842, built Dipford House and retired there, leaving Cutsey to his son, Thomas, who married in 1855. This Thomas Blake was responsible for most of the changes in field boundaries. About 1860 the huge brick barn, reckoned to be the largest in Somerset, was built. It was designed by John Watson of Torquay and was highly innovative. Fodder could be mixed in the three-storey centrepiece and distributed at loft level to the cattle sheds. Thomas's other claim to fame was that he is said to have caused a man to be put in the stocks for brawling in church, this being the last occasion on which the stocks were used (see page 46).

As well as Cutsey, Lipe Hill, and Georges, Thomas Blake owned Hersewell, which he left to his tenant, Mr Coram. Thomas Blake's sister, Mary Corner, and her sister Elizabeth had the Mission Room at Daw's Green built about 1890, and this they let to the Churchwardens at the nominal rent of 5s a year. Mary Corner's daughter, also called Mary, married Eland Clatworthy, an ironmonger from Taunton. He had already been married and had a son, Tom. Eland and Mary's first son was William Clatworthy, and after the estate was sold in 1941 he retained Cutsey and farmed it until the early 1970s. The planned construction of the M5 motorway right in front of Cutsey House was enough to persuade William and his wife Nancy to sell up and move to Long Sutton. To many of the older residents of Trull he was known as Bill Clatworthy, farmer, landowner, churchwarden and parish councillor. His departure marked the end of a remarkable dynastic period spanning over a quarter of a millennium.

The occupancy of the next owners, Richard and Ruth Eggins, only lasted a couple of years before it was again put on the market. The farm was sold in several lots so that the farm which the new owner, Gordon Hawkins, bought was somewhat smaller than when Bill Clatworthy had been farming it. Tragically the Hawkins family had only been at Cutsey for seven years when Gordon died. Following his death his family sold Cutsey House and built a new farmhouse and some farm buildings on the other side of the road, which they moved into in August 1984. In 1998 work began converting the farm buildings to residential. This included Thomas Blake's famous barn. Since 2000 Gordon's son Edward has been specialising in breeding and rearing Devon cattle, re-establishing a tradition at Cutsey. When Tom Clatworthy was killed in the Great War one of his obituaries ended with the words: 'It is hardly necessary to add that Mr Clatworthy (Eland) is one of the best known breeders of Devon cattle in the West of England'.

The west wing of Cutsey House dates from the 17th century. The oak staircase and the plaster ceilings in two of the rooms downstairs are probably contemporary with it, but the panelling is rather later in date. The imposing addition to the house was built by Thomas Blake and finished not long before he died, without issue, in 1880.

Steart Barn

STEART BARN

Sketches of the barn c.1950 showing the roof timbers

The word Steart means a tongue of land. Steart Barn was a combination of barn and linhay, but seldom used except as a linhay. It was built entirely of wood, the walls of the barn being of elm weather boarding. The wide eaves of the great roof covered the cattle stalls. In spite of its venerable appearance it is unlikely that it was built before the 18th century, as the timbers were saw-cut.

By 1975, when the two neighbouring fields were sold to Julian Pidgeon, there was no hint that Steart Barn had ever existed, so sometime in the preceding 25 years it must have fallen into complete disrepair and the site cleared. Mr Pidgeon built himself a house close to the site of the barn but this is not the first time there had been dwellings at Steart. Census records show two families living at Steart Cottages in 1891.

Hamwood

The name Zany was attached to the site of two old cottages on this farm, but the holding of Zany has a long history. In 1207-8 Algar of Sernege paid 1s to the Bishop of Winchester for not having his corn ground at the Lord's mill. At this time Sernege (Zany) was part of Holway, not Trendle. In the survey made shortly after the dissolution of Taunton Priory, the tithes of corn of Hamwood and Cerney were valued at £7 1s 4d. The reason for their being valued separately from the rest of the parish is obscure. In 1569 Henry Smyth, William Sherwood, with others of Woodland Tithing, provided three pairs of almain rivets (suits of armour), six bows, six sheafs of arrows, two bills, two skulls (brimless iron head-pieces worn by archers), a sword and a dagger to arm the local defence force. This Smyth was probably the holder of

Hamwood. In 1635 John Smyth of Hamwood had two seats in Trull church.

Before the middle of the 17th century Hamwood had passed from the Smyth family to the Bakers. In 1644 John Baker was one of the signatories of 'The humble petition of the Inhabitants of Trull desiring some reasonable allowance for quartering of souldiers of Lieutenant Colonell Powells Company' (see page 59). He was also one of the three 'Rators' who on 1st March 1654, were responsible for raising £4 19s within the parish, probably towards the support of the armed forces of the Commonwealth. In 1647 John Baker held 'one half yardland and two farthing lands of Bondland with certain parcels of Overland', for which he paid £1 6s 7d Lord's rent, more than anyone else in Woodland Tithing. The same year Botolph Thomas paid £1 for 'certain parcels of land called Serneys', implying that Zany was then a separate holding. James Wetham held 'parte of the Lord's Wood called Hamatt Wood with one cottage' and paid 10s 11d, while Edward Keene and Richard Skinner each paid 5s for parts of the same wood. In 1664-5 John Baker paid £1 6s Hearth Tax on 13 hearths, which would have included those in his cottages. He owned more hearths than anyone else in the parish, and was the only man described as a 'gent'. He died in 1677, and there is a memorial to him and his infant daughter in Trull church. The status of gentleman did not prevent John Baker, the son of this worthy man, from being fined 6s for swearing six times. The money so raised was distributed to the poor of the parish. In 1700 John Baker was only paying £1 Lord's rent for Hamwood. He or his son married Margaret Blake of Cutsey in 1709.

The farm had passed out of the hands of the Baker family by 1744-5, when Mr George Davey was in possession. That year Mrs Gale paid £1 Lord's rent for Hamwood Wood. The memorial to the Buncombe family in the north aisle of Trull church records the burial of Susanna, wife of Thomas Buncombe of Hamwood, in 1777 and of Thomas Buncombe himself in 1795.

In 1842 Hamwood was owned by John Hamilton and farmed by Thomas Gadd. Serneys had become Zanhay or Zaney by this time, and was part of Hamwood Farm. Later in the 19th century Hamwood was acquired by the Blakes of Cutsey. Trull Parish Magazine for January 1915 records that the two cottages at Zaney were furnished and ready for the reception of Belgian refugees, and the following month they had arrived and settled in. Mr Clatworthy had to demolish the cottages in 1939, but if he had waited another year the Germans would have saved him this expense, for a bomb was dropped on the site, which is now part of the M5 Services.

Hamwood Copse is possibly the only remaining piece of the woodland which must have covered a large area and given the tithing its name. In 1952 it was not part of Hamwood Farm, but of Little Hamwood. The oak and ash in the wood were formerly coppiced, but have been allowed to grow for many years. There are numerous rotten stumps and no natural regeneration of trees has been observed. The wood which is now part of Hamwood is now only 3.143 acres but a plan of the parish dated 1805 shows that it then included field 21, so that its area then was 15.786 acres.

Miss Hawkings of Sweethay Court, who was born at Hamwood, could remember four horses being used to turn the threshing machine. There was apparently little change in land utilisation between 1842 and 1952 when the Hawkings siblings put Hamwood up for sale. Failing to reach the reserve the farm was let to Hugh Grant who began cheese making, an innovation in the parish. This enterprise was to continue until 1995. The Grants bought Hamwood in 1964 and following the loss of 38 acres of land at Zany to the motorway services in 1974, they were able to acquire Westleigh Farm in Angersleigh. Hugh died in 1993 and his two sons, Graham and David, continued to farm Hamwood until they retired in 2008. The farm was then purchased by Charles Stanbury, who continued to milk cows but changed from Friesians to Jerseys. By 2015 this had become the last remaining dairy herd in the parish. Forty years before nearly every farmer in the parish would have milked cows. In 2019 Hamwood changed hands again. 210 acres were put on the market and it was bought by the Sparks family of Wellington. Hamwood is now occupied by Emlyn Sparks who continues to milk Jerseys.

Hamwood farmhouse may be early 17th century in date, although Julian Orbach[1] has suggested that it is the remnant of a late 17th century house. It has an unusual plan which includes a front range with a central doorway, approached through a combined porch and stair-block, leading into a cross-passage between two rooms, at the rear of one of which is a back-to-back stack between that room and a third room in a rear wing. There are ovolo mullioned stone windows set in brick (or brick-faced) walls, which makes the house an early example of the use of brick in Somerset. Over the front door are the Baker arms which also occur on the Baker memorial in Trull church. Internally there are moulded beams and a fine moulded fireplace, which was not discovered until 1965. At the same time the stone mullioned window in the same room had its sill lowered to provide more light. The rest of the windows underwent significant restoration in the mid-'80s. The original hipped roof has been replaced. In 1985 the listing was enhanced to Grade II*, one of only two in the parish with this grade, the other being Chilliswood Farmhouse and adjoining buildings.

Kibbear

It is known that Kibbear had been part of the Manor of Taunton Deane, as the sale notice in the *Taunton Courier and Western Advertiser* of September 1859 tells us that the two lots currently in the occupation of Mr Poole are customary freeholds of inheritance, parcels of the Manor of Taunton Deane. Twenty years after the disposal of the manor's land the hamlet of Kibbear contained five farms. Elizabeth Sykes owned Kibbear House and farmed 32 acres. Susannah Smith owned two farms of 56 acres each. The first one was farmed by Thomas

Buncombe, and the farm now known as Kibbear Farm was farmed by William Middleton junior. Susannah Smith also owned Lower Canonsgrove, which was 97 acres and farmed by Dinah Osborne though nearly 30 acres of this was at Kibbear.

Ten years on and Susannah Smith's two farms had apparently amalgamated and were being farmed by Charles Poole. Samuel Day farmed 20 acres and another holding of 68 acres was being farmed by John Woodberry. By 1881 Kibbear Farm was 180 acres and being farmed by Charles Spiller. He and his wife Mary had ten children, but when the youngest was born around 1877 there would be no more children born at Kibbear Farm for over 120 years. Charles and Mary's third daughter, Jessie, became Trull School's first pupil teacher in 1875 (see page 97). At 14 and for the next 4 years she was the only assistant to Harry Whale, the head teacher. In 1879, if every pupil had been in attendance, the two of them would have been teaching 145 children.

When Charles retired George, Edward and Petronella (known as Nellie) farmed Kibbear until George died at the beginning of the Second World War. The farm was auctioned on 6th July 1940 and consisted of Kibbear Farm, 107 acres, Higher Kibbear, 39 acres, and additional accommodation land of 18 acres. The farm was bought by Charles and Patrick Butler, both of Threadneedle Street, London, who, the following year, signed a tenancy agreement with Harold Small. Harold's notebook which he kept during the war years records many interesting facts and figures, including his motor fuel application for the months of May, June and July 1943 when he claimed 50 gallons to cover him for the 248 miles for milk deliveries, 150 for taking livestock to market, 64 for corn to and from the mill, 120 attending sheep and cattle away from the farm, 150 attending sales and meetings and 15 going to church.

After the war Mr Small was able to buy the farm from his landlords. In 1975, following the opening of the M5 motorway, Mr Small did an exchange of land with Vivian Helyar of Poundisford Lodge, whereby several fields of Mr Helyar on the north side of the motorway were swapped for a similar acreage belonging to Mr Small that had been stranded on the south side of the motorway. Harold Small retired in 1990, and the farm was sold to Peter Parris of Cutliffe Farm.

Kibbear farmhouse is an interesting dwelling of cob, brick and stone with slate roofs, the varying parts of which span three centuries starting with the cob section from the early 1600s. In 2008 the Parris family also acquired the land at Eastbrook which had been part of Hamwood. Along with land at Comeytrowe this made the Parris family the largest landowners in Trull, even though Cutliffe Farmhouse and buildings are just outside the parish boundary. Currently Kibbear Farm has been converted to form a large holiday complex. Richard and his family have moved back to Cutliffe, and Peter and his wife have built themselves a new farmhouse at the end of Kibbear Lane, next to their new set of farm buildings.

Reaphay

This holding dates back at least to 1327-8, when William of Reaphegh paid 7d tax to the Royal Exchequer, but practically nothing is known of its history. The land belonged to William Blake in 1842, and was farmed with Cutsey until 1942. The field boundaries are almost exactly as they were in 1842. The house appears to have been built in the 18th century or to have been remodelled then, and was used as two cottages before 1942.

Following the break-up of the Cutsey estate these two properties once more became a single residence, then owned by Michael and Bridget Roffe-Silvester. Michael was the master of the Taunton Vale Hunt and Reaphay Farm became the home of the kennels. These provided an invaluable service to the neighbouring farms as a depository for fallen stock. This however came to a tragic end in June 1996, when Michael's son John and his wife Kirsty were both killed in a head-on car crash returning from a night out. John was aged 44 and Kirsty 32. The other driver, Luke McKinley aged 18, was also killed. The tragedy was compounded by the fact that John and Kirsty's two young children were then orphaned. The youngest was just a baby and this had been John and Kirsty's first evening out together since the birth. The result of John's death was that the hounds moved to West Hatch and the farm was sold. The new owner was Cdr. Jeremy Hurlbatt RN OBE who served on the Royal Yacht *Britannia* in the 1980s, but during his time at Reaphay was running a couple of companies, one of which was the Rubber Rigid Inflatable Boat Company.

Spearcey Farm

At the start of the 19th century John and Mary Trood lived in this 17th century farmhouse where they had nine children. When the house was listed in 1988 it was suggested that alterations were carried out during their occupancy. By the time of the tithe apportionment, which for Pitminster was 1839, John and Mary had moved out and left many of the children still at Spearcey. In the 1841 census William Stocker Trood was registered as head of the family. John had moved to Higher Sweethay Farm (now Sweethay Court) which he rented from Frederick White. He also farmed the land north of Middle Sweethay which he rented from John Bevis. Cyril Green has calculated that John was farming 210 acres around Trull and Staplehay, though Spearcey itself was only 48 acres.

Twelve years later three sons, Richard, Robert and Samuel, and a niece Josepha, were at Spearcey. John, who was 80 by then, and Mary had moved in with their children at Spearcey, where John died the following year. In 1881 William was also back, where he died in 1892 which probably marked the end of the Trood dynasty at Spearcey, though Richard did not die until 1906. The Troods were both cider makers and maltsters with numerous orchards at Spearcey and the other holdings farmed by John. With a pony-powered cider mill and press at Sweethay it is possible that this is where they produced their cider. The malting was carried out at Spearcey and the malt house is still in existence.

The next family to live at Spearcey were the Porters. Edwin Porter was from Spaxton, where he had been farming 118 acres. He was a widower and had one son, William, who after marrying lived in Amberd Lane. Their son, Arthur, in turn lived at Spearcey. Arthur described himself as a farmer and cider grower, and he was entering orchards in Greenslade's annual apple auction.

In 1938 Arthur gave up the tenancy at Spearcey and William Rosewell, with his son Maurice, took over. They too appear to have sold most of their apples in the annual apple auction. William was a successful breeder of Dairy Shorthorns which he used to show at the Autumn Show and Sale at Taunton Market, winning the silver challenge cup two years running in 1944/45 and picking up reserve champion in 1946. In third place was SC French of Bathpool, who happened to buy Spearcey Farm when it was auctioned in December 1957.

Sidney Charles French, known as Charlie, ran a milking herd as well as rearing beef cattle and was, for a time, a partner in Fideoak slaughter house at Bishops Hull. In the early sixties and for the next two decades the two orchards to the north of the house were developed for housing, the loss of acreage being made up by a purchase of land at Poundisford when Vivian Helyar put it on the market in 1991. With a couple of other land purchases the total acreage of Spearcey Farm now stands at about 150. Charlie French's son, also Sidney Charles French but this time known as Sid, farmed Spearcey together with his son Guy. Their speciality was growing straw for thatch, an enterprise that entails the use of some really vintage agricultural machinery.

Sid was a well-known character who had served on the parish council for many years. In 2023 both Sid and his wife Wendy passed away leaving Guy to carry on the farm with the aid of his trusty farm hand Martin Fouracre, who is depicted in the photograph on p. 88 along with his colleague Alan Spiller.

Sweethay Court

Few references to this farm have been found before 1904, when a Sale Catalogue shows that it was then known as Higher Sweethay and included Hither and Middle Slippery, Home and Cobbs Meadow, Croft and Shutes Meadow, and the cottages now known as Higher Dipford.

This land was owned by Frederick White junior, and farmed by John Trood in 1842, but the name Sweethay was not then attached to the farmhouse now called Sweethay Court. This is a 17th century house, much altered in the 19th century. In the barn on the right of the picture are two cider presses, as well as the old machine which is entirely hand-made, and was used to work the cider mill. It has not been used for at least a hundred years but is still in remarkably good condition.

In the second half of the 19th century Higher Sweethay Farm was farmed firstly by Robert Hewett and then by his widow, Emma and son Francis Denning Hewett. After the change of ownership in 1904 the house was, in the words of Cyril Green, 'drastically altered' and converted to a private residence with its current name of Sweethay Court. When the Hawkings retired from Hamwood, Grace, Henry, Hubert and Harold all moved to Sweethay Court. Grace died the following year and when Hamwood was sold on 29th September 1964, Hubert died the following day and Henry the following year. In 1968 a stained glass window at the back of the south aisle in Trull church was dedicated to the memory of the Hawkings family. Sweethay Court lost its last semblance of being a working farm when the land and the wagon house, on the opposite side of the road, were sold off following Harold's death on 15th October 1973, and the land to the south of the house was sold by the subsequent owner, Keith Tinning. These two fields were acquired by the Lock family of Middle Sweethay

Farm. They had moved there in 1944 and still farm there now, though the farmhouse has also become a private residence. Since the departure of the Hawkings, Sweethay Court has changed hands several times. When David and Maria Hedderwick moved there in 1996 they built a large extension to the west end of the house. David died on Valentine's Day 2014 and the house has since changed hands again. The name Higher Sweethay Farm has now been given to properties at the east end of the hamlet.

Middle and Lower Sweethay Farms
The farmhouses of these two farms are both on the south side of Sweethay Lane and within a stone's throw of each other. In Sweethay Lane is Middle Sweethay farmhouse, a grade II listed medieval house, with a 17th century extension. It was described in the 1942 sale particulars as a picturesque and comfortable farmhouse built principally of stone and cob with plaster faced walls, and slated, thatched and galvanised roof. In anticipation of the house's listing, and the limitations that would have placed on any subsequent alterations, the remaining section of thatch was later replaced with slates.

Next to it is a short lane that leads to Lower Sweethay Farmhouse, another medieval house. Traditionally the lands of Middle Sweethay were north of Sweethay Lane and the lands of

Lower Sweethay to the south. At the time of the tithe apportionment in 1839 Middle Sweethay was 61 acres, owned by Revd Hugh Helyar and occupied by Thomas Hine. Lower Sweethay was 44 acres, occupied by Reuben Bicknell and owned by his mother, Susannah Bicknell, who was living just down the road at Boxenhedge, the location for a school boarding 11 children. Over the course of the next hundred years occupants came and went in quick succession with Middle Sweethay being offered for sale in 1910, 1917 and eventually in 1942, at which point both farms appear to be under the same ownership, namely that of Mr JT Cridge who was farming Lower Sweethay Farm and living in the farmhouse but letting Middle Sweethay to a tenant. The estate was offered for sale in three lots, Middle Sweethay containing 30½ acres, Lower Sweethay, 58 acres and land, buildings and two workmen's cottages totalling 44 acres.

Austin and Linda Lock bought lot 1 and with their seven children moved in to Middle Sweethay Farmhouse. Since the initial purchase several more fields have been acquired bringing the size of the farm to about 77 acres. Austin and Linda had three more children at Middle Sweethay; Lesley, Linda and James. Clifford, who was two when they moved, contracted polio as a child which left him severely disabled. For many years Clifford could be seen leaning on the garden wall where he would chat to passers-by. Clifford passed away in 2006 and ten years later Jimmy had a heart attack and also died while out working. This left Les and his son and Jimmy's two sons farming Middle Sweethay which had then been in the Lock family for 75 years. However, Jimmy's widow, known as Kat, then put her share of the farm on the market and it was bought by the Parris family.

When the estate was sold in 1942 Lower Sweethay was bought by Mr GE Osborne who farmed it till 1954 when it was again put on the market. The sale particulars for that sale described it as a very attractive small dairy farm extending in all to about 44 acres. In the early 60s Lower Sweethay ceased to be a dairy farm when a Miss Done established a stud at the farm. This operated till 1987 when the farm was again auctioned. By now the farm had shrunk to 21.79 acres and was bought by Mr and Mrs RA Hughes from Ascot, Berkshire. The property came with a barn with planning consent for conversion. This barn along with one other has now been converted to residential. If one includes Lower Sweethay Farmhouse currently being two dwellings, then there are now over a dozen properties on these two farms.

Trull Green Farm
This name is a recent one. The farm was known as 'Buces' in 1842, when it was occupied by John Stephens. Some of the field names are two or three hundred years old. Pope's Nine Acres contained Pope's Four Acres in 1842, and Mr William Dawe had a holding named Pope's in 1744-5. Bonny Five Acres was Boney Five Acres in 1842, and there were two holdings named Bonnings in 1744-5. Among the other field names are Claypitts, Joices Four Acres and Bradford Meadow. The last name dates back to 1635, when Christopher Stutt had

a seat in Trull church on behalf of Bradford's.

On the gable end of the projecting wing of this L-shaped thatched and stone-built farmhouse, which has several mullioned windows, is the date 1637, with the initials RS MS beneath. The only man with the initials RS who held a seat in the church in 1635 was Richard Skinner, who was one of the churchwardens for that year. In 1647 he was paying 7s 3½d lord's rent for one farthing of bondland in North Trendle Tithing.

The wing is an extension to the main range. This range has a traditional vernacular 3-room and cross-passage plan and probably dates from the 16th century or even earlier, and may originally have included a medieval open hall. Remains of an early jointed-cruck roof indicate that the range has subsequently been heightened, perhaps to allow for the insertion of an upper floor, which is also suggested by changes in floor levels on the upper floor.

In 1922 Trull Green Farm was purchased by Robert Seymour Hewett. Members of the Hewett family had been farming in Trull and Pitminster as early as 1812 when Chilliswood was bought by James Hewett, Geoffrey Hewett's Quaker great grandfather. He also rented Coxes Farm and moved with his family to Higher Sweethay Farm in the 1840s. Robert Seymour Hewett's son Robert Morley Hewett continued to farm Trull Green and in turn Geoffrey Smerdon Hewett farmed it. When in 1973/4 Somerset County Council compulsorily purchased enough acres to build a school, Geoffrey bought a farm in North Curry and transferred the milking herd there. The school project was cancelled and the land was sold on for residential development. When in 1994 Barton Green was developed Trull Green Farm effectively ceased to be a working farm, though Geoffrey remained in the farm house until his death on 14th November 2012. Geoffrey joined the RAF in 1945 serving for three years in Hong Kong and Singapore. On returning to the farm he had a spell as Regional Vice Chairman of the National Farmers' Union. He was a parish councillor and chairman of the Parish Council for many years. When after his death a new sports pavilion was erected in the George V playing field, it was felt appropriate to name it The Geoff Hewett Pavilion to commemorate a lifetime of service to the community.

Reference
1. Julian Orbach and Nikolaus Pevsner, *The Buildings of England: South and West Somerset* (2014) p. 645.

15   The School

There was a school in Trull over 130 years before John Wyatt's Charity School, described below. In 1623 Christopher Harries, the parish clerk, was presented at the Court of the Archdeacon of Taunton 'for keping of schoole without licence'. The case was dismissed, Harries paying 4d and 12d the latter possibly for the licence. Nothing more is known of this school.

John Wyatt of Trull died in 1755, and a quotation from his will reads: ' I give unto my said dear Wife Prudence Wyatt and unto my Brother in Law Thomas Welman Esqr the Revd Mr Farnham Haskoll and Isaac Welman Esqr and Simon Welman Gent both of Poundisford the full sum of Two hundred pounds of lawfull money of Great Britain which I request and desire that they will lay out in the purchase of an Estate so as that the clear yearly Rent and profit thereof may be applyed and disposed of to and for teaching and instructing as many poor children of the said parish of Trull without any distinction of parties as my said Wife and other Trustees or their successors shall after the death of my said Wife but as my said Wife alone shall during her life think fit and convenient to read, and for buying Bibles and other usefull Books to be Given and Distributed unto and amongst such or any other children of the said parish of Trull as my said Wife during her life and my said other trustees and their successors shall think most proper for their instruction in the true principles of the Christian Religion and advancement of piety there'.

The 'Estate' mentioned in the will is two fields then called Lower and Upper Hoges, which the Trustees let to farmers, using the income to run the school and buy the books. Lower Hoges is now the King George V Playing Field, and Upper Hoges became post-war council housing named Wyatts Field in his memory. The Governors of Trull School still present a 'John Wyatt's Bible' to school leavers going on to secondary education at the end of each school year. Thus started about 1755 John Wyatt's Charity School, which was held in a two-storey building in the churchyard, near where the War Memorial now stands, with accommodation for the teacher in charge. It was almost certainly the old Church House where in the later Middle Ages the parishioners held church ales to raise money for their church (see page 123).

A small record book dated 1755 in the Somerset Heritage Centre names two mistresses in the Charity School, Sarah Harman and Betsey Wrangrove (or Wrantmore), and 17 children are listed. In 1870 school attendance was made compulsory by Act of Parliament. Trull was the nearest elementary school for some 130 children aged between five and ten. It was clear that the school in the churchyard could never accommodate such a large number. The site for a new school was given by Ambrose Lethbridge of Eastbrook House, and opened in 1875.

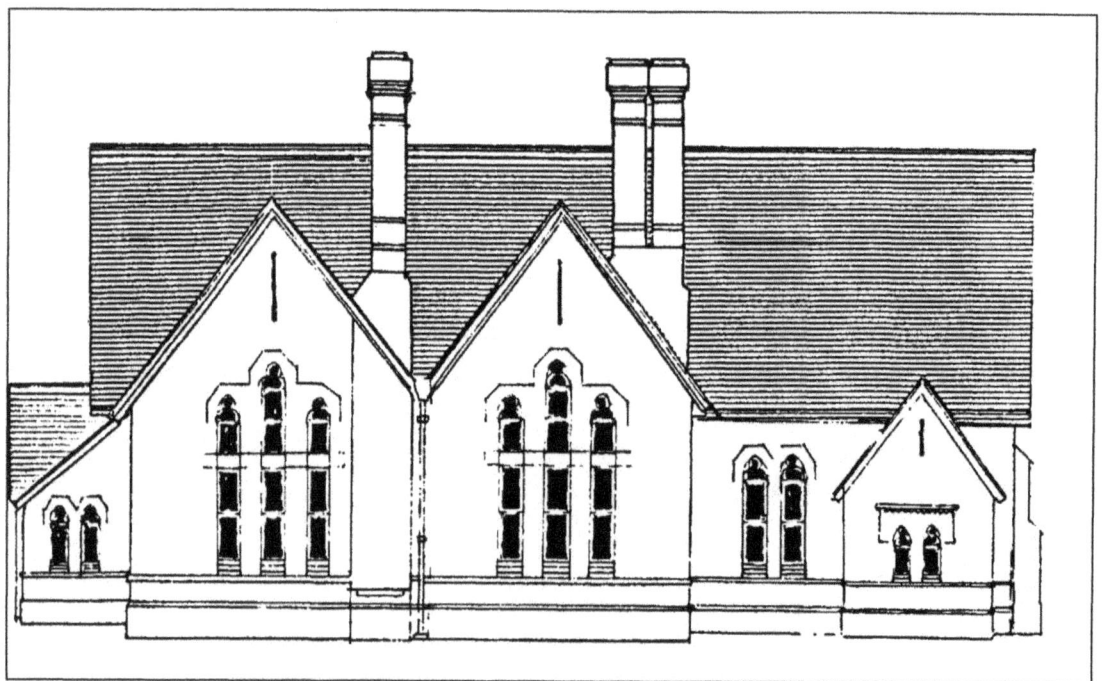

The school in 1885, showing the schoolroom, infants' cloakroom, new classroom and boys' cloakroom.

In 1873 Harry Whale had been appointed as master. Previously all the teachers whose names we know were women. He started keeping a logbook in which the day-to-day events of school life were recorded at the end of each week. Trull's headteachers continued to do so, and fascinating extracts from the early logbooks were included by Cyril Green in his history as an appendix (see Reference on page 102). In recent years this has been replaced by a weekly Newsletter.

The school children used to get money prizes for regular attendance, 5s for the top class down to 2s for infants being given for full attendance. Mr Whale, though strict in school, was a kindly man, who used to let the children off early to go into Taunton to watch the procession when there was a circus coming to the town. Mrs Jefferys Allen of Gatchell House used to give pancakes to the children on Shrove Tuesday, and her butler was never taken in by the girls who exchanged hats in the hope of getting a second pancake.

In those days, children attending paid, according to a resolution of the school managers, 1d per week if residing in Trull and 2d if residing in Pitminster. The 'three Rs' seem to have constituted the curriculum, and evidently punctuality was insisted upon, for we read that late comers were made to sweep the schoolroom and do extra lessons in the dinner hour. There is no mention of any physical training, and much absence is recorded, for bad weather, bird scaring, harvesting, potato lifting, and baby minding. Needlework, however, seems always to have been a feature of the girls' work.

In 1875 the Managers appointed Jesse Spiller, a farmer's daughter aged 14, to help as a pupil teacher, and for the next five years this was all the assistance that Mr Whale had, though by then the number on roll had reached 145. In 1880 a Government Inspector recommended the appointment of an assistant, and two years later an assistant mistress took up post.

Mr Edwin Denning of Lower Comeytrowe Farm was one of the Governors of the Trull National School, and when his daughter Kate married William Harry Elphinstone in 1883, the school children were given a holiday. The schoolmaster told them to be sure to go and see the wedding, as it would probably be the last time they would ever see postilions.

By 1885 another classroom and a much-needed porch for hanging clothes had been added to the building, and for the first time we read of a school treat and an entertainment in aid of the Band of Hope. By 1890 the Managers had instituted a library, and a second assistant or pupil teacher had been appointed; and in 1895 a great highlight seems to have been a 'Phonograph Concert', each child paying 1d to attend. In 1902 a teacher was granted leave to go to London to witness the Coronation procession of Edward VII, and Coronation mugs were distributed to the children. The school building was enlarged in 1903 with a separate cloakroom for the girls and infants. An entertaining entry of this year tells us that 'a better way of cleaning slates is to be tried, by tins of water and rubbers, instead of by breath'.

The year 1908 seems to have been eventful. A needlework inspection took place, a flagstaff and flag were presented to the school, purchased by the parishioners, and Empire Day was appropriately celebrated, the children afterwards being presented with buns, oranges and ginger beer. We also read of the master being absent in town to discuss the formation of a cookery class for the girls. Two years later the older children were taken to Taunton to hear the Proclamation of King George V, and a week's Coronation holiday was granted. In 1912, with the coming of a new master, various forms of handicraft were introduced into the curriculum, as well as gardening, and cookery classes in the lower room of the Men's Club. We read also for the first time of medical inspection and a visiting school nurse and dentist.

A few years later there was a further enlargement of the building, although even as late as 1920 we read of 75 children being taught in an unpartitioned room. From 1922, with the coming of a new Headmaster, Mr EW Groves, the school became more modern and progressive in its outlook. Several improvements in the building took place, gardening with beekeeping was made a speciality, and woodwork classes for the boys were begun.

The Second World War had a direct impact on the school. Some 80 children and their teachers were evacuated from Ilford and West Ham and billeted locally. Since the school had only four classrooms, some had to be taught in the Parish Rooms (demolished in 2013 and replaced by the Trull Church Community Centre) and the Baptist Chapel in Comeytrowe Road, subsequently converted into a house (see page 112). In May 1944 a group of local women, with Council assistance, started to provide the children with hot midday meals which they cooked and served in the Village Hall (also demolished in 2013).

In 1956 all the boys and girls aged 11 to 15 were transferred to Priorswood, the new secondary school in Taunton, and Mr Britton, the then head, and his deputy, went with them. With the departure of the older children, Trull was left with just over 100 pupils aged 5 to 11. But the population of Trull and Staplehay was growing rapidly, and many families with young children were coming to live here. By 1971 the school roll had reached 175. The photo on page 98 shows the school from the church tower before the changes of the 1970s.

In 1970 the present hall was built, and for the first time the whole school could assemble, concerts and plays could take place, and the midday meals could be served. It was also equipped as a gymnasium for physical education. Two new classrooms were added in a single storey block at the back with, for the first time, inside toilets. Team teaching was the education fashion at the time, so the new classrooms were open plan. Unfortunately, the two teachers concerned were as different as chalk from cheese, so the Trull School Association (the PTA) had to raise money to buy heavy curtains to separate them! Eventually these were replaced with a permanent wall.

At the same time, the old school play shed was converted into a heated indoor swimming pool, in which the younger children were taught to swim, with the parents providing the money and much of the labour. The older pupils were taken each week to the St James' Baths in Taunton. At weekends and school holidays parents could borrow the key and supervise their children using the pool. But by 2010 the maintenance costs had become too great, and the space was needed for an additional classroom. This is now called The Pool Room, and a blue carpet shows where the pool used to be.

In 1976 the second phase of remodelling took place. A new floor was built within the lofty roof space of the original schoolroom. For the first time the Head and school secretary had separate offices (they had previously shared a study upstairs in the Parish Rooms) and there was a staff room with toilets separate from those for the children. And in 1993 a new floor was built above the 1970 single-storey classroom block, providing two new classrooms and a new library. The splendid painting of it on page 99 by Trull's resident artist Ted Milligan, who had designed the extension as an architect with Barnes Canon, was kindly donated to the school.

In 2005 a new entrance with disabled access and a new reception area were added. It incorporated the Headteacher's office, a staff room and toilets. The names of all the headteachers since Harry Whale in 1875 are displayed in the brickwork. They were all men for more than a hundred years until, in 1984, Margaret Jones was promoted from deputy. Since then they have predominantly been women. And in 2014 Yew classroom block was built, incorporating two classrooms and toilets currently used by the Year 6 children. In 2023 there were 258 children on roll, in 8 classes, all named after trees.

In 1958 the County Council had bought part of the allotments which then lay between the boundary wall of the school and the playing field as a grassed area for the school. This was enlarged in 2014 when the new pavilion was built on the playing field, and the school leased the triangle of land behind it from the Parish Council to use as an 'outdoor classroom', now known as the 'forest school'. The access to the playing field is through a wrought-iron gate which celebrates the late Queen's Golden Jubilee in 2002.

In 1886 Trull School had entered into union with the Church of England National Society, and ranked as a 'Church School'. From 1902 onwards, Somerset County Council assumed the responsibility for paying staff salaries, providing materials and equipment, maintaining classrooms and playground. Since 1956 Trull School has been a Church of England Voluntary Aided Primary School. This means that the school Governors are responsible for the outside of the buildings, and have to find a proportion of the cost of any improvements, with help from the Diocese and ecclesiastical charities.

Trull School has always had a close association with All Saints church. For many years the Rector was the Chair of the school governors, and is still an ex officio governor. The foundation governors, nominated by the church, are in a majority. In recent years the church's Children & Families Worker has been the School Chaplain.

Trull Pre-School, now held in the Trull Church Community Centre, started in 1971 as Trull Pre-School Playgroup in the Old Village Hall, as described in the Parish Archive's publication *Where We Used to Meet*. The school is one of the beneficiaries of the Trull Parish Lands Community Fund (see Chapter 13) which incorporates the John Buncombe Stocking Charity for children of Trull School.

Reference
CW Green, *A Short History of Trull School 1755 – 1997*.

16 Queen's College

Queen's College took its present name in 1897 as a tribute to Queen Victoria in her Diamond Jubilee year. But it was founded in 1843 by William French and James Barnicott, two prominent lay townsmen, as the West of England Wesleyan Proprietary Grammar School. Thirty-three pupils were enrolled, and the school occupied Castle House, restored in recent years, in the courtyard of Taunton Castle. At this time, the old Taunton Grammar School was in decay, and the social cleavage between Church and Chapel was at its peak. Methodists therefore took the lead in providing education for their sons in their own school. Queen's was the first Taunton college and grew rapidly, so that by 1847 it moved into its present Tudor-styled building in Trull Road with over 100 boys.

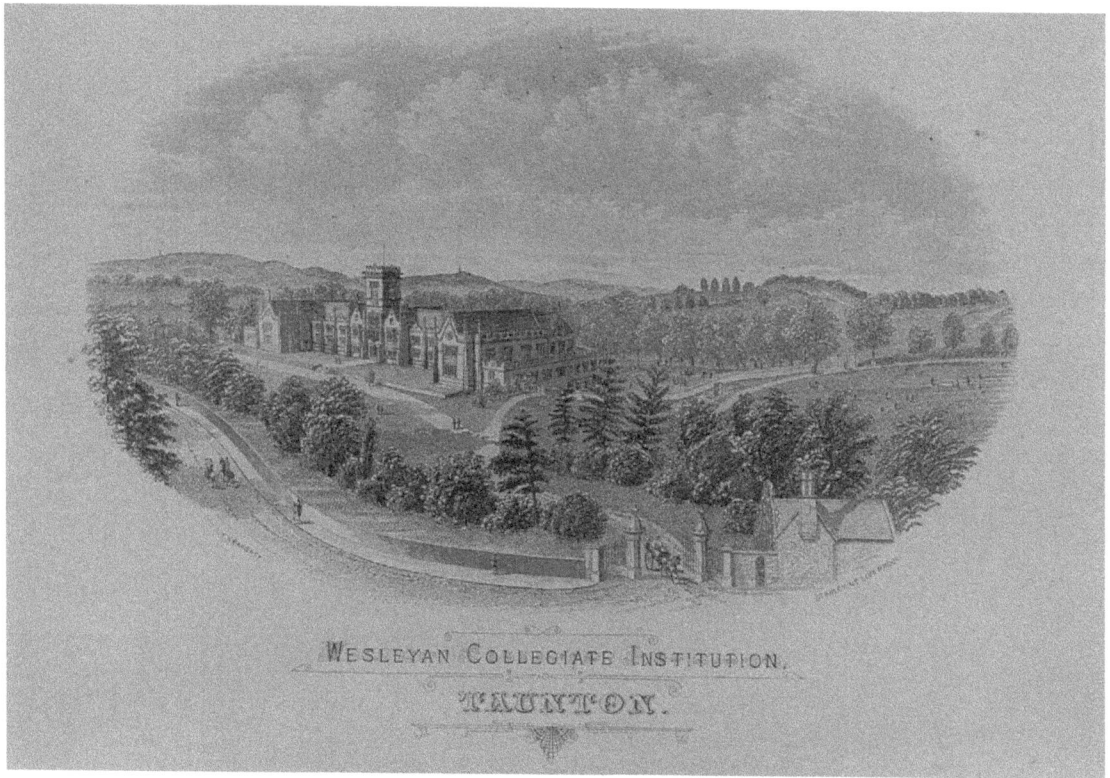

Since then the buildings have expanded, with the bridge and library (now known as the Old Music Room) being added to the school in the 1920s. This addition was built in commemoration of those who served in the First World War. Several local properties have been bought as boarding houses. The first, in 1862, was 'for boys whose parents were willing to pay extra for comforts not enjoyed in the main building'!

The College was founded in the Wesleyan Methodist tradition. At the opening ceremony in 1843, the *Somerset County Gazette* reported the Rev Richard Ray as stating: 'The grand object would be, whilst the boys placed in this seminary were instructed in science and literature, to teach them also plain and uncorrupt Christianity'. The present prospectus states that: 'Queen's College is a member of the Methodist Independent Schools Trust. The Methodist Church is engaged in education as part of its Christian mission in the world and schools in the group aim to extend the Methodist ethos and character and contribute to diversity in education'. The College has always had close links with Temple Methodist Church in Taunton.

London University, founded in 1833, conferred degrees without religious tests, unlike Oxford and Cambridge. Queen's was quick to exploit these opportunities, became affiliated, and incorporated into its school crest the University arms, alongside Taunton Castle and Wesley's Wyvern. The latter is now the College's logo. Since the 1970s the school has been co-educational, with both female and male boarding houses. The school now incorporates nursery, pre-prep, Prep, and senior schools.

In the past the school has had strong links to Trull church. This was particularly so during the 1970s and 80s, when Arthur Birchall was Head of Queen's Junior School and also a Reader at All Saints. Junior School boys used to periodically attend the family Services, led there by David Sharpe (see photo from the mid-1980s). Junior School Carol Services were held in the church; on one occasion a longstanding churchwarden tried to turn away a suspicious-looking long-haired stranger, until the pupils convinced him that this was in fact their art master.

For many years Senior School boarders could choose between Temple Methodist and Trull church for Sunday services; from the 1980s services were more often held in the College Chapel. Trull church had the advantage of a shorter walk and also the presence of older girls in the choir! The boys left their mark on some of the Trull church pews and their carved initials can still be seen there. Joint confirmation services were held where pupils were confirmed as members of both the Anglican and Methodist churches.

The children of several vicars and rectors of Trull have attended Queen's College, and this too was reflected in links between College and Church. In recent years these links have diminished, except for older students who have been involved locally on community projects. After heavy snow in 1978 the senior boarders distributed milk around the village. And more recently a group assisted with the restoration of the mill leet, which was much appreciated.

The College had purchased Trull Meadow in the 1970s in anticipation of needing it as an additional playing field. In the event this never happened and in 2020 the College put it up for sale, citing the possibility of long-term housing development. This caused great concern in Trull, and the Trull Meadow Trust was formed to try and raise funds to purchase the site. The College governors were sympathetic to this outcome, and eventually the Trust was able to purchase the Meadow to protect it in perpetuity (see page 134).

17 Juliana Ewing

From June 1883 till May 1885, Juliana Horatia Ewing lived with her husband Alexander at Villa Ponente in Trull Road, now part of the Mountbatten Nursing Home. She was a prolific writer of stories and poems, chiefly for children. These appeared initially in *Aunt Judy's Magazine for children*, which her mother started in 1886 and named after her daughter, before being published as books.

These became extremely popular and gained her a wide circle of friends and admirers. Roger Lancelyn Green called her works 'the first outstanding child novels', Rudyard Kipling claimed to know one of them almost by heart, and another admirer of her work was E Nesbit. They were said to make grown men weep! A talented artist herself, her works were frequently illustrated by such notables as George Cruikshank and Randolph Caldecott. Her story *The Brownies* gave the Baden-Powells the idea and name for the junior level of the Girl Guides, and the Brownie Guides still use her story today. Trull Parish Archive has an almost complete set of her books, and a copy of the biography written by her sisters. These may be borrowed from the archive (ask at the Church Office in the Trull Church Community Centre).

Jackanapes and *The Story of a Short Life* were her best-known books. The only one she wrote whilst living in Trull was *Mary's Meadow*, a story with an underlying theme of gardening and beautifying waste places, which was inspired by her wrestling with the wilderness of a garden she found at Villa Ponente. In it, Mary searches for a rare variety of cowslip and attempts to grow it in a neighbouring field. This reflected Juliana's passion for the cultivation and preservation of old English garden and wild flowers.

Its publication and popularity led to the formation of the Parkinson Society, named after John Parkinson, King's Herbalist and author of *The Garden of Pleasant Flowers* published in 1629. Its objects included 'to search out and cultivate old garden flowers which have become extinct, and to plant waste places with hardy flowers'. To her delight, Juliana was invited to be its first President. She began, but was never able to complete, *Letters from a Little Garden*, giving children advice on planting and growing garden flowers.

Her husband, Alexander, had a career in the Army in the Commissariat and Pay Departments, eventually rising to the rank of lieutenant colonel, and had many overseas postings both before and after their marriage. But his true love was music, which he had studied in Heidelberg. His most famous composition was the tune to the hymn *Jerusalem the golden*. He claimed to have composed it whilst boating with a friend on a lake in Killarney! On his return home he took it to the Harmonic Choir in Aberdeen, of which he was a member, and it quickly caught on. It has been known as 'Ewing' ever since.

Juliana's health deteriorated, and after two unsuccessful operations she died of cancer in May 1885 at the age of 43. She was given a military funeral and buried in Trull churchyard, under the yew beside the stocks. The grave was covered with the mass of flowers sent by her many friends and admirers. On her tombstone is carved one of her favourite flowers, a double primrose.

After her death, her sister arranged that the many donations 'which are being sent to me from distant countries, as well as from readers of my sister's books who live near home' endowed a cot at the Convalescent Hospital, Highgate, in Juliana's memory. And in 1899 a memorial stained-glass window in the north aisle of Trull church was dedicated to Juliana and Alexander's memory by their nephews and godsons.

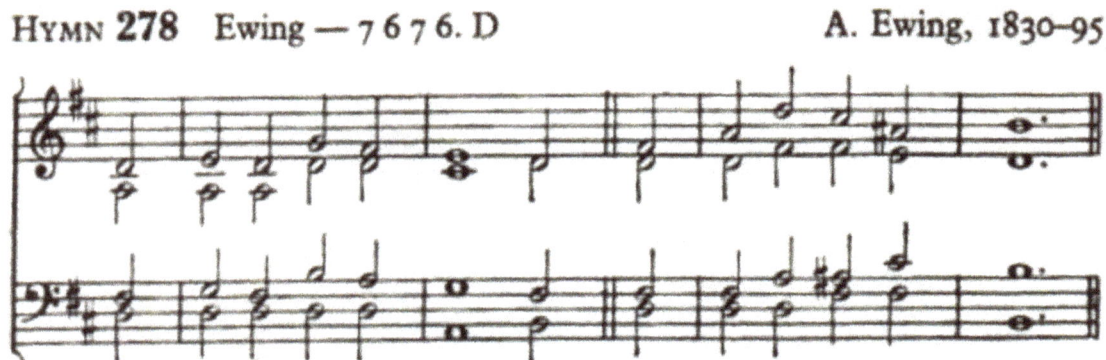

18 Victorian Memories

A comparison of Map II with Map I in the original edition of *The Story of Trull* (see our Preface) emphasises the purely rural character of Trull village in the early years of Queen Victoria. Some readers will be able to find out from Map II the names of the fields on which their houses were built. Many Victorian memories have been recalled elsewhere in this book, and the object of the present chapter is to build up a human picture of village life in the second half of the 19th century.

The broadsheet transcribed below throws a good deal of light on the personalities of the 1870s and must have caused a great stir when it was circulated in the parish in May 1871. This is only the first four verses – the following twelve are even more scurrilous! If you would like to read the complete original, together with notes identifying the people referred to, it is reproduced in the first edition of *The Story of Trull*, which can be borrowed from the Parish Archives. It was, not surprisingly, anonymous, but 'the author is said to be a man named Lane'.

SELLY'S DOGMAS

In a neat little Cottage, not far from Trull Green,
There lives a fine Parson as ever was seen,
He thinks himself great as a King on his perch,
His name you may guess – he's a man of High Church.

The first thing he wanted, I've heard people say,
Was to have a fine pulpit, made just his own way.
He offered a Warden, to pay him five pound,
To have the old carving and pulpit pulled down.

But no – said the Warden – that must not be done,
I never will yield to your dogmatic fun,
This beautiful carving the Church doth adorn,
And I'm sure it will last for ages unborn.

His reverence then flew in a horrible pat,
Bolted out of the Church and put on his hat,
Went home to his Wife, as straight as a rocket,
The fiver, or note, he put back in his pocket.

'Selly' was the vicar at the time, Rev HC Seller (see page 33). He had previously been vicar from 1854-1857, and returned to the living in 1863. The replacement of the pulpit was included in a faculty granted in that year. But this was prevented by the churchwardens of the time, elected by the church members in preference to the vicar's nominations, for which we living in 'ages unborn' must be very grateful.

In 1866 George Hayes, the sub-postmaster, was also a boot and shoe maker; Thomas Hewett a carpenter lived at Cox's; there were two blacksmiths, one in Trull next door to the general shop, and one at Daw's Green; there was a wheelwright, a butcher, a baker and two other shopkeepers. Batts Park was known as Batts House, and Miss Mary Ann Passmore kept a 'ladies school' there, though it had been given up by 1883. The Misses Ann and Sarah Pratt ran a boarding and day school for young ladies, but this seems to have gone by 1875.

Roads were originally the responsibility of the parish that the road ran through, with able-bodied men required to give six days a year to do road work. But by the beginning of the 18th century they were in a very poor condition. So from 1707, by Act of Parliament, Turnpike Trusts were set up to improve them and charge users a toll to cover the cost, like the two Severn toll bridges used to do. They slowly covered the country, and by 1840 around 1,000 Trusts covered some 20,000 miles. The Taunton Trust turnpiked what are now the Trull and Honiton Roads in 1752. The local toll house was at the junction of Wild Oak Lane and Trull Road, close to where Red Tiles was built in the early 20th century. The late David Marks remembered that "in the 1960s, my old Gran still talked about the Honiton Road as 'The Turnpike' ".

Beside the turnpiked Honiton Road stands a milestone. Situated at the junction with Wyatts Field it is a listed (protected) structure, one of nearly 50 in the parish. It was erected in the early 19th century, of local stone and cast iron with raised lettering. In 1876, the Taunton Turnpike Trust ceased to exist, as road maintenance had become the responsibility of local and national governments.

The *Parish Magazine* of the 1880s shows that about 90 people belonged to the Provident Club, and each received a bonus of 7s 6d in December 1887. There was also a Blanket Club; blankets were distributed for the winter, and washed and brought back for the summer. The Temperance Movement had many adherents. The following is an extract from an account of a meeting of the Band of Hope (to teach children the importance and principles of sobriety and teetotalism) in 1887. 'An unusually interesting meeting was held on Wednesday evening, Nov 16th, when Miss Amy Dening kindly addressed the children in a very impressive manner, giving striking instances of the terrible misery caused by drink which have come under her own notice'.

Glencoe and Fairview Terraces in Wild Oak Lane and Oakfield Terrace in Church Road were built in the early 1880s on land then part of Carter's Orchard, and South View Terrace later. They were built of yellow Taunton brick, the first houses in Trull to be wholly built of this material. More than a hundred years later the planning authority insisted that the Gatchell Oaks development in the Honiton Road be built to match this as the 'Trull vernacular style'.

A number of handsome Victorian villas have survived, such as Amberd House, Canonsgrove House, Eastbrook House and Lodge, Gatchell House, The Bell House, Quintons and Spy Post House. Others have been demolished for housing developments and only the gate piers show where they were – Claremont (now Coplestons) and Southwell Lodge (now Southwell).

Reference
CW Green, *TRULL and STAPLEHAY with an eye on the past.*

19 Religious Nonconformity in the 19th and 20th centuries

Fulwood Independent chapel in Pitminster (formerly Presbyterian but described as Congregational by 1914) originated in 1705 and a record of baptisms for 1802-36 includes some references to families living in Trull, and parts of Pitminster parish now in Trull, who presumably attended the chapel. For example, on 5th February 1809 Mary, daughter of William Govier, labourer of Daws Green, and Mary his wife, was baptised, as was Abraham, son of William Govier, labourer of Comeytrowe, and Mary his wife on 3rd March 1811 (presumably the same family at a different address); and on 16th April 1809 Charlotte, daughter of William Fouracre, carpenter of Eastbrook in Pitminster, and Mary his wife, was baptised.

Baptists were active in the neighbourhood by 1885. Records of Silver Street Baptist church in Taunton refer in 1891 to 'cottage services' at Staplehay. In 1894 Staplehay was recognised as a 'preaching station' of Silver Street church, and it was decided to secure a room for the services which had hitherto been held in a cottage. Instead, however, it was announced in January 1895 that Thomas Penny had purchased land in Trull on which to build a chapel (for £300) as a branch of Silver Street, although seating and other fittings would have to be paid for by subscribers, and the chapel would be held in trust for Silver Street by the Baptist Union Corporation. The chapel formally opened on 27th June (see photo below) although Penny was unable to speak through hoarseness. It was reported that attendance at Sunday services during July was 'most encouraging'.

Penny had also offered to pay for the addition of a vestry, which may be the origin of a small extension at the rear of the building which has recently been removed. In 1914 it was intended that a Sunday school be built in the open space on the east side of the chapel, but this came to nothing, probably because of the outbreak of war.

This post card shows Trull Baptist chapel between the houses of South View in Comeytrowe Road, not Comeytrowe Lane as indicated by the caption. During the Second World War the chapel was used as overflow for evacuee children at Trull School. Only the older ones could go there, because the smaller children could not see over the pews!

The small chapel in Comeytrowe Road survived until the 1960s. In the 1950s the chapels (or 'village causes') at Corfe and Trull were supervised by the Revd LJ Egerton Smith as associate minister (to the pastor at Silver Street) until his death in 1958. A memorial fund in his name was set up in 1959 'for funding part of Trull chapel for children's work'. Efforts were then made to appoint an assistant minister to take over the chapels at Halcon, Corfe and Trull, but no suitable appointee could be found, and in 1961 Halcon withdrew from the combined scheme.

In November 1961 there is mention of redecoration and drainage work at Trull chapel, and to the purchase of a moped for 'Sister Phyllis'. She had taken over responsibility for Corfe and Trull chapels, and in 1962 moved into a flat in Corfe provided by Silver Street church. In

September it was reported that furniture and floor covering had been purchased for Trull Sunday school from the Egerton Smith memorial fund. In January 1963 blizzard conditions prevented services at Trull and Corfe, but in February Sister Phyllis announced that she was starting a Bible class at Trull. She continued in her work until invited to join a church at Erith in 1965, when Mr PW Smart, secretary of Trull chapel, agreed to conduct two services a month there.

In September 1965 it was reported that a Harvest Thanksgiving had taken place at Trull and that the Sunday school was 'progressing favourably'. In March, Mr EO Lawrence reported on the need for more Sunday school teachers for the 50 children, which he repeated in October and in January 1967, together with an appeal for more cars to take children to and from the chapel.

The chapel at Corfe had now closed permanently due to lack of support, but in June 1967 Mr SB Woodford, who was already working for Trull chapel, said that he was willing to become lay pastor at Trull if a manse were provided for him. Silver Street was only willing to provide an honorarium, however.

In May 1968 it was reported that 'women's work' in Trull was successful but that Sunday congregations only numbered four or five people and there were 15 Sunday school children. Silver Street therefore decided to transfer the Sunday School to the new Youth Centre in Galmington, and to arrange a monthly Sunday evening service in Galmington for a trial period. From January 1969 the Galmington services, which functioned as an 'outreach' of Silver Street church, continued until July. In that month it was decided that 'Miss Hewitt' could use Trull chapel for a monthly Women's Meeting for another six months, although Silver Street intended to ask the Baptist Union Corporation to authorise the sale of the building.

Trull chapel, with the adjoining land, was sold by auction on 24th April 1971 for £4,250, which was to be invested by the BU Corporation and the income paid to Silver Street church. An application to turn the building into a dwelling was approved in that year. The conversion was carried out with little or no regard for the chapel's architectural features, which had included red brickwork with pale banding, tall 2-light windows in Italianate style (echoing those at Silver Street) and a circular window in the front gable above an entrance porch.

References
TG Crippen, *The Story of Nonconformity in Somerset* (1914).
SHC, D/N/tau.b 4/2/3 & 4/2/7 Minutes of Silver Street Baptist church 1880-1897 & 1955-1979.
SHC, T/PH/pro/67g Microfilm of Somerset Nonconformist records including Fulwood

20 Butcher, Baker …

In the 19th century, we can see from county directories such as *Kelly's*, from the census returns, from baptism registers which record the fathers' occupations, and later from adverts in the Parish Magazine, that even a village like Trull had a wealth of local trades. Travel, even as far as Taunton, was something of an undertaking in those days for many people, so was not embarked upon for a weekly shopping trip. Hence the local tradesmen had to provide pretty well everything for their customers.

Butchers

So let's start with butchers. We know that there was one in Trull in 1866, but we don't know his identity. But we do know that in 1904 Hazeldene, the very substantial red brick house now 7 Church Road, was built for Frank Day. He and his older brother George established themselves as G & F Day, butchers at Pitminster and Trull. One of the front rooms became the butcher's shop, a shed behind was used as a slaughterhouse and the land behind as pasture for animals subsequently killed.

Telephone: Taunton 165 Y 3.

G. & F. DAY,

Family Butchers,

Pitminster & Trull. Also on Saturdays, 13 and 14, Taunton Market.

Purveyors of Best Quality English

Beef, Mutton, Pork, Veal & Lamb, Corned Beef, Pickled Tongues, Home Cured Bacon, Pork Sausages, &c.

FAMILIES WAITED UPON DAILY.

'Families waited on daily' meant calling at houses for orders and then delivering meat over a wide area. Charlie Day ran the family business with his mother after his father Frank died in 1926, and when she died in 1948 he became the sole proprietor, moving from the Thatched Cottage on Trull Green to Hazeldene. Subsequently, a large room at the side of the house became a general store, selling groceries, fruit and vegetables. He was very active in village life, being Chairman of the Parish Council for many years. He retired in 1971, and the house and business were bought by Gerald David and then Neil Matthias. The latter eventually applied for planning permission to convert the drive beside the house into a car park, and, when this was refused, he sold the house as a residence and moved to Minehead. Michael Collard then opened a butcher's shop which included fruit and vegetables in part of 1 Church Road, now the Pilates Studio. When he eventually moved to Mountfields Road in south Taunton, he took orders and delivered meat for sale at Trull Stores for some years.

Post Office

The first Trull Post Office occupied the front room of 1 Honiton Road, and the first telephone in the village was installed there. George Hayes, sub-postmaster in the mid-19th century, was a shoemaker, and his successor, Albert Bull, a plumber. When the Revd Bonsey moved from the Old Vicarage to the New Vicarage in Wild Oak Lane in 1908, the wooden hut he had previously used as a garden study was moved into the garden of 1 Honiton Road and became the new Post Office, as shown in the photo.

Until after the last war, letters were sorted by the sub-postmaster at Trull and delivered by bicycle. In 1964, whilst Mr & Mrs Richards were sub-postmasters, the wooden hut was replaced by a stone building brought from Blagdon Hill, which has been the 'Just Hair' unisex hairdressers since 1981. In 1967 the new building at the end of Church Road, now the Pilates Studio, was taken over by Mrs Terndrup to sell drapery, tools, DIY and garden requisites. When she became sub-postmistress, the Post Office was moved to part of this building, the rest being her 'Handy Shop'. Finally, in 2015, the Post Office moved to its present location in Trull Stores, after modifications to make it fully accessible. It left behind the Post Box, which since 2012 had been painted gold by the Royal Mail to mark the gold Paralympic medal won by Debbie Criddle in equestrian dressage at the London Olympics.

Shops
Trull Stores

The village store dates from at least the mid-19th century, when Edward Jones opened a grocer's shop beside his smithy. His sister-in-law, Mrs Jane Johns, ran it from the 1880s until her death in 1911, her daughter Elizabeth until she retired after the Second World War. The original entrance was in a passageway beside the shop (now part of 3 Honiton Road), as depicted by Ted Milligan. The shop and smithy were eventually converted into one in 1936 - the smithy was the part of Trull Stores which extends farthest back from the road.

Trull Stores has had a succession of owners. Many people remember Dee and Ray Luke and their son-in-law Neville with particular affection. In those days it was still an old-fashioned shop with a long counter in front of which customers queued, whilst Dee served several of them at the same time! When they retired in about 2010, the new owner converted it into the self-service shop it is now. And then in 2015, Sandra and Cherry Philips absorbed the Post Office (see page 117).

The Corner Shop
This has changed hands and usage many times over the years. In the early 20th century it was a dairy, and its owners had a milk round. Complaints were made to the Parish Council that water, used to wash out the milk churns, ran down the ditch at the side of the road, causing a disagreeable smell in hot weather. In 1927 Bessie Shire turned it into a general shop. Then it was used by the owners of the adjacent garage to sell odds and ends of motor accessories, such as cans of oil. In recent years it has been a hat shop, an insurance office, an arts and crafts business, a sausage shop, and a deli.

Staplehay too had a general store in the 1960s and 1970s, on the right as you turn into Sweethay Close. It was built as Mace – Staplehay Stores. In part of the same building was Anthony's Hair Stylist. But the shop increasingly struggled to be viable, particularly as supermarkets opened in Taunton, and eventually it closed and was used for storage. Then Paddy Bakker, with the help of a substantial National Lottery grant, converted it into a Spinners and Weavers Workshop, which it has remained ever since.

Garages

In 1927, Stanley Shire set up the Corner Garage, complete with a petrol pump, at the end of Church Road. This was in direct competition with his brother Ernest who, in partnership with Arthur Doble, ran a garage in the former smithy beside Trull Stores just two doors away. Then in 1936 Doble and Shire moved to their new purpose-built Trull Garage beside Trull Green. They advertised cars for hire, and a 20 seater motor coach. This was frequently hired to transport the Sports Club football, hockey and cricket teams when they had fixtures away, and the church choir and bell ringers on their annual summer outings. After the war, coaches became a major part of the business, which ran five or six at the highest point. To keep them covered when not in use, two war-time Nissen huts were purchased, and rebuilt on 3ft high walls to give the required headroom. These can be seen in the aerial photo, kindly donated by Keith Shire, who grew up there. It was used as a Christmas card to their customers. It is dated to the mid 1960s, by identifying the brands of car shown in the garage and on the road.

The garage and the surrounding forecourt now house several small car sales and repair businesses. The Corner Garage changed hands a number of times until the present owner, Nick Mayled, took over the business and renamed it the 'Owl Garage'. Since 1995 Tim Dedman and his son Simon have leased it.

In 1936 Ted Bowerman set up his first garage in a workshop by the Crown Inn at Staplehay, with its petrol pumps on the pavement outside. The business continued to grow after the last war, and in the 1950s he bought the extensive plot of land between the Crown and Rose Cottage. The road-side showroom was progressively enlarged to its present size, and two houses built beside it. It has remained a garage ever since, now Staplehay Auto Services, although it no longer has petrol pumps.

Pubs
The Winchester Arms
A map of 1838 shows the Winchester Arms building as a row of four separate cottages with a fifth in what is now the car park. This seems then to have been the home of Samuel Loosemore, described in the census returns from 1841 as innkeeper. In the course of the 19th century the fifth cottage seems to have been demolished, and the other four joined together to form the present Winchester Arms, named after the Bishops of Winchester, the former lords of the Manor of Taunton Deane. This has been the village pub ever since.

The Crown Inn
This was a pub in the centre of Staplehay from the 19th century. For many years after the

First World War the landlord was a member of the Bowerman family. From the 1930s Cyril Bowerman was landlord for 44 years. But in the present century it increasingly struggled, and eventually the owners were given planning permission to convert it into three properties.

The old inn sign from the front of the building was rescued by the Parish Archive Group, and is in storage until we have a Trull Museum!

Other occupations
There was a host of other trades in the parish, known from the Census returns that include 'occupation', from adverts in the Parish Magazine and local papers, and from reminiscences

of older residents. These included several builders, such as G Fouracre and Sons in Mill Lane and the Lock brothers at Fairlawn Coach House at the beginning of Dipford Road; two cobblers, Mr Lentall at Eastbrook and Mr Venn in Lilac Cottages, Church Road; several smiths including John Chilcott at Daw's Green; a wheelwright and waggon maker at Boxenhedge; and two undertakers, Mr Browning at Staplehay and Mr Doble at Glencoe Terrace. Countless women did dressmaking, and many took in laundry, particularly widows.

In the post war years many examples of agricultural diversification could be found in the parish. There were numerous cider makers, a cheese maker, Anne and Robin Leamon ran a plant nursery at Chilliswood and Sidney French produced straw for thatching. In addition there were several farmers and their wives running Bed and Breakfast establishments. As we enter the third decade of the 21st century nearly all these businesses have passed into the realms of history. However, if one was inclined to visit our village there is no shortage of self-catering holiday accommodation, and whilst here why not call in at the 'Hive cafe' in the Trull Church Community Centre, where a warm welcome is always guaranteed.

21 Halls and other amenities

The first recorded mention of a village hall in Trull goes back to 1526, when the churchwardens' accounts refer to 2s 6d being paid in rent to the lord of the manor for the 'chyrch howse' (see page 48). A fine example of a church house, and one of only two in Somerset that are still used as public halls, can be found at Crowcombe, dating from 1515. Situated in the southwest corner of the churchyard, Trull's church house was a two-storied building used for celebrations known as 'church ales' to raise money for the church. It could also be hired for private events. In 1755 the trustees of the John Wyatt Charity (see page 95) opened their school for poor children in Church House. This school was replaced in 1875 and the old school used for a carpenter's workshop until, in 1886, the old school plus one or more cottages and a stable were demolished. While the demolition was in progress a sketch was made of one of these buildings by Edward Jeboult (see page 45). In the annotation to the sketch, the original of which is held by the Somerset Heritage Centre, Jeboult refers to the building explicitly as 'the ancient Church-House of Trull'.

As soon as the stables in the churchyard had been demolished they were replaced on a site across the road, northwest of the school yard. This development also included a coach house, and nine years later a fine chert and tile two-storey building was added which became known as the Parish Rooms.

When opened by the Bishop of Bath and Wells in January 1896 it was referred to as The New Men's Club and Parish Room. This building consisted of a kitchen and a room on the ground floor and two further rooms on the first floor. The Men's Club used the upper rooms, one of which had a billiard table. Prospective members had to be coached in playing billiards to ensure the green baize wasn't damaged. The lower room, although initially a reading room, was soon requisitioned by the school and here the girls were taught cookery. As school numbers fluctuated the extent to which the Parish Rooms were used by the school also varied, peaking in 1941 with the arrival of the evacuees and again in the 1950s as a result of the 'baby boom'. Later on, John Gifford (headmaster 1968-1984) had his office in the upper room, but in 1976 the school was expanded, and the Parish Rooms reverted to church use.

The Parish Rooms had never had pretentions of being a village hall. Ever since John Wyatt's School moved into the Church House, the village had to rely on the school for larger meetings, dances etc. This situation changed in 1920 when an ex-WWI army hut was acquired. It was transported from Salisbury Plain, and erected behind the Parish Rooms on land donated by Miss Wigram of King's Gatchell.

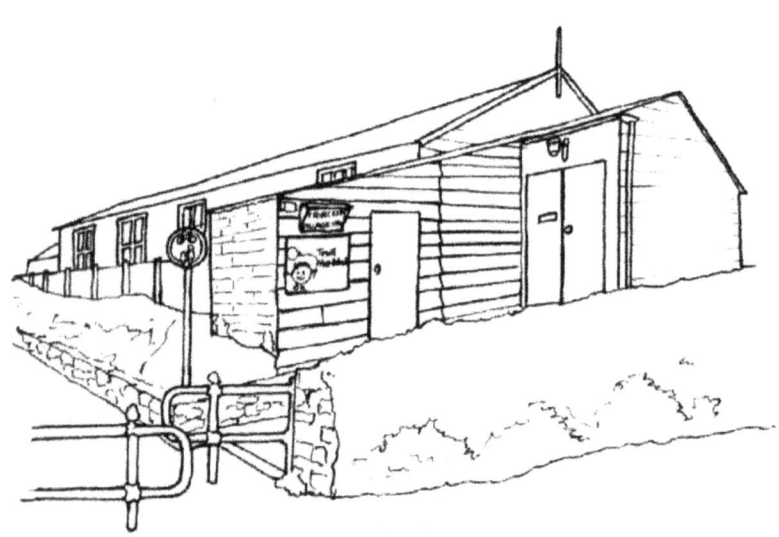

The whole project cost £300 and was ready for its grand opening on 6th January the following year. The Vicar, the Revd ML Winterton, performed the ceremony after which there was a whist drive and dance. He had envisaged the hall being available for 'literary and scientific lectures, musical society, whist drives, dances etc'. In practice, it was the venue for a wide range of village events, and it also provided new premises for the Men's Club. In 1925 a skittle alley was added along the Pook Lane side of the Hall. In May 1944 the school started to make use of the hall following the introduction of hot school dinners. Initially these were cooked and served in the hall, but later on they were centrally prepared and delivered. This arrangement continued until 1970 when the school was able to use its own newly built hall as a dining room. This freed up the Old Village Hall for the creation of the Trull Pre-school Playgroup.

For a number of reasons the Old Village Hall was far from ideal for a pre-school. Being a wooden structure meant that it was hot in summer and very cold in winter, and was serviced by inadequate heaters. Also the pre-school shared the hall with other groups, and so at the end of each session all the equipment had to be stored away and the hall cleaned, a task that would take staff and helpers up to an hour to complete. In spite of these disadvantages the pre-school continued to operate successfully until the hall's demolition prior to the building of the new community centre. A more detailed history of both the Parish Rooms and the Old Village Hall can be found in a booklet produced by the Trull Parish Archive Group entitled *Where We Used To Meet*. This is available for loan or purchase from the Parish Archive.

In July 1945 the Trull Welcome Home Committee was formed. A fund was established and three welcome home parties for returning ex-servicemen and women were arranged that were held in the Village Hall. Each invitee was presented with a Savings Certificate to the value of £4 10s (about £155 at today's value in 2023). In the Parish Archive (reference TPA/M War Memories) there is a list of attendees and background information on some of them.

It was planned that the fund would also go towards the erection of a Memorial Hall. This project was abandoned when a suitable site could not be found. However, the idea was revived in 1956, when the Trull Parish Lands Charity sold the land that had been let to the Trull Allotments Association to the village for £180 (£3,600). Somerset County Council agreed to construct an access road that would serve both the new hall and the school. A new committee was formed, and fundraising resumed with the aim of raising the £3,200 (£64,000) that it would cost to build and equip a village hall. Two grants were received, £6,577 from the Department of Education and Science and £1,645 from the Taunton Rural District Council. The rest of the money collected came mainly from a Supporters' Club Lottery, which at its peak had a membership of 540. Subscriptions were obtained at a rate of 6d per week over a period of 8 years by a loyal group of two dozen collectors, and a grand total in excess of £1,700 was collected. In addition the committee organised an annual fete which brought in on average £200 per year. The five fetes that took place from 1959-1964 were not just any ordinary event, they included a gymkhana and carnival procession that started at the Crown Inn, Staplehay. On 9th July 1960 the fete was opened by the then famous film star Miss Deborah Kerr.

The fete field had until recently been the property of Major Alexander Gould Barrett, nephew of John Chard VC of Rorke's Drift fame. On 12th March 1954 Major Barrett was involved in a road accident and died in Musgrove Park Hospital. Outliving his brothers, he had inherited the family estate late in life, and donated Burrow Mump at Burrowbridge to the National Trust as a memorial to the men and women of Somerset who gave their lives in the Second World War.

Trull Memorial Hall was opened in March 1965 by the Rt. Hon. Lord Merthyr, Deputy Speaker of the House of Lords. In attendance were the vicar of Trull, the Revd Derek Evans, the chairman of the Trull Parish Council, Mr KJ Burge, the chairman of the Trull Memorial Hall Committee, Mr FW Marston and the chairman of Taunton RDC, Mr George Lee JP. In the inaugural dance held the same evening, Sid Roberts and his Band provided the music.

At about the same time as the Memorial Hall project was progressing, there was also a conception of a scheme to provide a playing field for the village. This too had a faltering start. The original idea derived from a wish for a national memorial following the death of King George V in January 1936. In the November of that year a King George V Foundation was set up, the object of which was to promote and assist in the establishment throughout the United Kingdom of Playing Fields for the use and enjoyment of the people. In Trull a Playing Field Committee was formed. However, in September 1951 it was reported that the committee had resigned due to lack of support. The Trull School children still desperately needed a playing field, so a reduced scheme was suggested whereby an acre-and-a-half of Trull Meadow would be purchased from its owner Mr Drew. As this was never planned to benefit the village as a whole, grants to help finance this scheme were limited. The committee expressed disappointment that the full scheme, which gave space for adult cricket and football grounds and a selection of other amenities, should have been given up. They were in no doubt that the full scheme was the right thing for the village, but they felt that they could do no more than hope that it would become practicable at some future date.

The committee's hopes were eventually realised. A grant of £600 was received from the National Playing Field Foundation – hence the name King George V Playing Field - £75 from the Somerset Playing Field Association, £236 from the Ministry of Education and £125 from a legacy that had been left to the Trull Sports Club by Mr Edmund Hulland. Additional funds were still required, so a New Year's Eve Social and Square Dance was held in the Men's Club Hall charging 2s for adults and 1s for children under 15. As a result the Lower Hoges field was purchased from the trustees of the John Wyatt Charity in 1956 for £560, and the new playing field was opened on 13th June 1959. After an address by Mr Kenneth Burge, the Chairman of the Parish Council, the former vicar of Trull, Prebendary CW Trevelyan, was invited to perform the opening ceremony. This was carried out by raising the Union flag at the entrance to the field. Both the flag and the pole had been donated by Prebendary Trevelyan to commemorate the occasion.

The Memorial Hall celebrated its Silver Jubilee in 1990, and the occasion was marked by the building of an extension. Writing in the *Parish Magazine*, the Memorial Hall Committee Secretary, Mrs Rosemary Crane, was able to keep parishioners up to date with the progress, starting with a fund-raising Grand Concert held in the hall on Saturday evening 12th January 1991. The music was provided by Nancy Beverage (Soprano), Simon Hurrell (Tenor), Ron Tickner (Piano), Steve Graham (Lute) and The Chandos Brass Ensemble. In March she wrote 'Our Annual General meeting is on 3rd April at 7.30pm. in the Hall and we shall be pleased to show our plans for the extension to anyone interested. The County Council has now promised us a grant, and it is hoped to start work at the end of July'. Her entry for the September issue read: 'Steady progress is being made by Messrs Pearce on the building of the extension, which it is hoped will be ready by the end of this month. The committee were pleased to note how careful Pearce's had been to cause as little disturbance as possible to the running of the Hall'. Pearce's were rewarded by having the extension named the Pearce Suite. Pearce Construction had also been responsible for building the New Rectory in Wild Oak Lane in 1992, which according to their site poster was for 'The Diocese of the Bath & Wales' (*sic*) see photo overleaf.

By the end of the millennium Trull was still blessed by having the benefit of three halls, but all three had seen better days. The Old Village Hall had undergone some refurbishment in the early 1950s but now was dilapidated and its upkeep expensive, requiring a subsidy from the Memorial Hall account. The Parish Rooms had a serious damp problem necessitating the permanent use of a dehumidifier. And circa 2003 a full structural survey carried out on the Memorial Hall concluded that although it could be expected to have a life of up to 30 years, the insulation and the heating system were inefficient. It was also believed that the hall had insufficient capacity. A plan was therefore drawn up to demolish the Old Village Hall and sell the site for development which would then support the rebuilding of the Memorial Hall. The estimate for the rebuild was £1.18m. Unsurprisingly this scheme did not obtain universal support, and in September 2006 it was deemed not to be feasible. The urgency to find a resolution to the Hall's problem was intensified by the inadequacy and poor state of repair of the Parish Rooms. Hence this was now considered to be a community problem, and as a consequence of this the Trull Community Centre Development Group, under the chairmanship of Barry Bloxham, was formed.

The Group comprised representatives from the principal village bodies, namely the Memorial Hall, the Parochial Church Council, the Parish Council, the School and the Trull Action Plan Group which had produced an informal Trull Parish Plan in 2005.

Work started immediately discussing the merits of some 17 different options, before arriving at a scheme to build a community centre on the land currently occupied by the Old Village Hall and the Parish Rooms. There were issues regarding the ownership of the land that Miss Wigram had donated for the Old Village Hall in 1920, and in September 2010 a formal meeting was held for all Trull residents which unanimously approved of the proposal. At this point much of the initiative passed to the Parochial Church Council which commenced planning the new centre. After planning permission was granted tenders went out, and CG Fry was appointed as main contractor.

All that was required now was to raise somewhere in excess of a million pounds that the project was going to cost. Although the Parochial Church Council felt unable to apply for lottery funding, they were well placed to obtain grants from a number of other agencies. Sums were raised from the community in the form of pledges and donations and other fund-raising initiatives, a fine example of which was sponsored abseiling down the church tower which was led by the rector, Adrian Youings. Work on the building commenced in August 2013. Early progress was slowed by poor weather conditions, but by October the following year when the photograph overleaf was taken from the church tower, the centre was ready for its official opening. For this miraculous achievement the Bishop of Bath and Wells, the

Rt Revd Peter Hancock, spoke at a service of thanksgiving in the parish church. This was followed by the cutting of a ribbon, the ceremony being performed by Barry Bloxham in the presence of the rector, both of whom had worked tirelessly to create what even the most sceptical had to concede was a wonderful new facility.

In the same year as the Community Centre was opened, Trull Parish Council were the beneficiaries of a section 106 agreement between the developers of Amingford Mead, off Amberd Lane, and the Taunton Deane Planning Authority. Normally these are works carried out by the developer to offset the impact on the community and improve the local infrastructure. However, in this particular case the agreement needed to reflect the fact that the land on which the 30 houses were to be built was designated as 'Vivary green wedge'. As can be imagined, when the planning application was registered in April 2012 it generated much opposition, and a group calling themselves 'The Thin Edge of the Wedge' was formed. The opposition eventually fell short of taking a case to judicial review and the developer, West of England Developments Ltd under the leadership of Andy Lehner, put forward a package of contributions to benefit the community.

These were a field that would double the size of the adjacent George V Playing Field, plus another 4¾ acre field situated between the waterfall and Amberd Lane. This had originally been called Headweir, and from 2014 the Village Field, but in 2022 was renamed the QEII Field in memory of the late Queen. Before the war it had been used by the Trull Sports Club (see page 140), who had been offered the tenancy of the field and a pavilion by Mrs Bayly of Amberd House. As part of the section 106 agreement Mr Lehner also offered to improve the car park in front of the Memorial Hall, and to build a pavilion in the northwest corner of the playing field. This was an offer the Trull Parish Council could not refuse, so with their support the application was approved.

Mr Lehner had already built a number of pavilions in villages in the locality. Generally intended as cricket pavilions, the design could be tweaked to suit individual requirements. As Trull's cricket club pitch was situated on Dipford Road, Trull's pavilion would be used by the uniformed youth organisations and exercise and wellbeing classes, as well as private hire for children's parties and the like. The pavilion was named after Geoff Hewett, a long-serving Chairman of the Parish Council. More information on Mr Hewett can be found in the section about Trull Green Farm on page 94. There was no formal opening, presumably because, unlike the other facilities, it was not the culmination of years of fundraising by any village organisation. But David Marks' article 'Just a thought' in the December 2014 issue of the *Parish Magazine* suggested that readers should make the effort to go and have a look at the magnificent new red brick sports pavilion, replacing the old decrepit changing room building.

The hedge between the existing playing field and the adjacent field was removed so that they became one. Improvements such as an all-weather perimeter path and outdoor gym equipment were provided. At the same time, the area of the playing field behind the new pavilion was leased by the Parish Council to Trull School as an 'outdoor classroom'.

Then in 2023 an extensive upgrading and expansion of the facilities was funded by £100,000 of the Community Infrastructure Levy from the sale of the first houses in the Orchard Grove development (see page 143) in the north of the parish. This income ceased in April 2023, when Orchard Grove became part of the new Taunton Parish (see page 6). An avenue of cherry trees was planted at the bottom of the field, funded by a £2,000 lottery grant for tree planting in celebration of the late Queen's Platinum Jubilee. In September 2023 the development of the playing field was recognised by being named by the Somerset Playing Fields' Association as 'Playing Field of the Year'. The Trull park was 'particularly commended for its immaculate presentation and provision of play and sports facilities'.

22 The twentieth century and after

Parish Nurse

At a public meeting in October 1920 it was decided to obtain the services of a parish nurse, paid for from the Marke and Norman Charities (see page 71). In 1922-3 the nurse paid 2,440 visits to patients. This lasted until the early days of the National Health Service which started in 1948. By then Trull, Pitminster and Corfe were sharing a nurse, and an Infant Clinic was

held in the Parish Rooms, where orange juice and cod liver oil were handed out. In 1950 this was replaced by a Child Welfare Centre organised by the County Health Department, which dealt with children up to the age of five, with a doctor in attendance. Transport was provided to and from the Clinic for those who lived at a distance. It was a great success, as much for the social side as the medical. The photo is of one of the Children's Clinic Parties at the Vicarage, in 1957.

Village Green

Trull Green, beside the Honiton Road opposite Trull Garage, may be all that is left of a village green, formerly known as Cockshayes Green, which once stretched to the Dipford Road. Before the last war there were orchards on both sides of the green. Children played cricket there in the summer, and in the autumn piled up wood for the village Guy Fawkes bonfire on 5th November. This only ceased when Doble and Shire opened their new garage opposite and set petrol pumps on the forecourt!

In 1961 the Parish Council was asked by the local authority to confirm that Trull had two village greens – Trull Green, 0.4 acres, and Boxenhedge Green, 0.13 acres, where Dipford Road forks either to Angersleigh or Daw's Green. But when they checked, a bungalow had been erected on Boxenhedge Green! There was no doubt it had been common land - the Taunton Deane Enclosure Act of 1851 had confirmed the allotment of the green to the inhabitants of Trull 'as a place for exercise and recreation'. It seemed that the land had been hedged so that it could be used as the parish pound, for detaining stray cattle until their owners could collect them. During WW2 everyone had been urged to 'Dig for Victory', so the owners of the adjacent Boxenhedge Farm had planted potatoes on the green and then fruit trees. Then in 1955 they had successfully applied for planning permission to build a dwelling on it. There had been no local objections, but clearly the local authority had not checked its own records properly. The bungalow when completed was descriptively named 'Three Corners'.

This early 21st century aerial photograph of the property is reproduced by kind permission of the current owners, Mervyn and Virginia Roach. The then owner was keen to sell the property, but with its legal status uncertain that was impossible. Eventually, following advice from various national official bodies, the owner agreed to pay the Parish Council £200 (worth in excess of £4,000 today) to be spent on the maintenance of Trull Green, in return for which the Secretary of State would 'extinguish' the rights of Trull residents to use it as common land. It was a very unusual situation, technically a 'purpresture' i.e. a wrongful appropriation of land subject to the rights of others, and was reported in the national Parish Councils Newsletter as a warning to others. So Trull Green is now the only common land in the parish, and is maintained by the Parish Council. Until recent years it was fringed by rare black poplars, but these became unsafe and had to be replaced by donated trees, joining the splendid red oak and sycamore beside the south wall.

Trull Meadow

Trull Meadow is not common land, but it is in public ownership. It has always been pastureland, with a public right of way across it. It was bought by Queen's College in the

1970s with the intention of using it for sports pitches, but it was never needed for that purpose. So in 2020 it was offered for sale with the possibility of housing development in the long-term, despite it having protected status in the Trull Neighbourhood Plan of 2017 (see page 143).

In order to prevent this, Trull Meadow Trust, now a registered charity, was set up to 'purchase Trull Meadow for the long term use and enjoyment of the village and the general community'. Local residents were invited to make a donation or an interest-free loan, grants were sought and fund-raising commenced, to meet the purchase target of £150,000. There was an enthusiastic response to this appeal, and by 2023 sufficient funds had been raised to complete the transaction. The Friends of Trull Meadow had been formed in 2021 'to offer practical help in the maintenance and other requirements of the Meadow', and in 2023 Trull Parish Council made the sum of £20,000 potentially available for infrastructure improvements to the Meadow.

The veteran oak in the meadow, on the right in the photo beside the parish allotments, is estimated to be 500 years old. So it would have been a young tree on 10th May 1645 when 7,000 Parliamentary troops quartered overnight in the fields of Pitminster, Poundisford and Trull before advancing the next day to relieve the siege of Taunton in the Civil War. Sadly its offspring, on the left, grown from an acorn and planted in 1953, was blown down in the November 2021 storms, but a replacement oak has been planted there. A similar incident had occurred more than a century before, in 1910. The photo shows Mr Whale, Headteacher at Trull School, and his pupils. The photo is included by kind permission of Nick Chipchase, himself Trull born and bred.

Flooding

On 10th July 1968, a deep depression led to the equivalent of two months rainfall in the Taunton and Bridgwater area in 24 hours. There was widespread flooding, not least in Trull, as the Sherford Stream burst its banks. New mown hay and tree branches had been swept into the stream and clogged the bridges at Eastbrook and Mill Lane. A touring caravan parked at Haygrove Farm was swept away. When the farmer, Arnold Lynas, attempted to recover it with his tractor that too was swept into the stream and he was lucky to survive, being saved by a stout branch and a courageous lady neighbour. Eventually the footbridge linking the mill to Trull meadow gave way, releasing the build-up. Water several feet deep flooded the Winchester Arms and a number of cottages.

The photo shows the clear-up in Trull the following day. A local 'Appeal Fund' was set up to give practical and immediate help to those most affected, and the Rural District Council also set up a fund to help the 315 homes affected in its area. It could have been worse. In 1960 Taunton town centre had been flooded (see the photo on page 77) and the £750,000 Tone Valley flood prevention scheme, although not finished, seems to have saved the town in 1968.

Uniformed Organisations
Scouting

There are no records of when Scouting began in Trull. The *County Gazette* for 17th July 1909 included an appeal for 'a Scout Master in Trull for an established Troop of three patrols'. The first record of a village Scout is on a small white cross in the churchyard, just to the east of the War Memorial. Burnett Govier, aged 11, died in February 1914 of typhoid after drinking stream water. Sometime earlier, he had been on duty with other Scouts, patrolling the Blagdon Hill reservoirs. Tension had been mounting in the months before war was declared, and ironically the Scouts were watching out for the possibility of German agents poisoning the water supply. The Government officially recognised the Scouts and employed some 20,000 in guarding railways, telegraphs, bridges and waterworks.

At first the Trull Scouts met in the school room. Then in December 1914 the *Parish Magazine* reported that 'the BP (Baden-Powell, their founder in 1907) Scouts distempered and renovated Rats' Castle and Mr Wakefield renewed the thatch and gate'. This was a disused cottage, long since demolished, beside the Sherford Stream to the south of Amberd Bridge. By 1931 they had moved to the annexe of the Crown Inn at Staplehay (converted into three housing units some years ago), and in 1938 to the former coach-house adjoining the Parish Rooms, in turn demolished in 2013 to make room for the Trull Church Community Centre. Since 2014 they have been the principal tenants of the Geoff Hewett pavilion. They are a thriving group, with sections for all ages, from Squirrels Scouts to Explorer Scouts. In recent years they have widened their membership to include girls.

The St George's Day Parade in Taunton is a traditional highlight of the Scouting year. Here is the Trull Group in the mid-1980s led by David Marks (see Acknowledgements. Photo courtesy of Somerset County Gazette).

Guides

Girl Guides date from 1910. Girls were keen to join the newly established Boy Scouts, but Robert Baden-Powell decided that a separate organisation would be best, and asked his sister Agnes to form the Girl Guides. The First Trull Group was formed in 1958 and met in the Parish Rooms. As well as the weekly activities, there were District camps and local ones, often on farm fields. There were also opportunities for Guides to act as messengers at the Royal Bath and West Show at Shepton Mallet, spending four days and nights there. One year they had a float in the Taunton Carnival.

In 1967 the younger Brownies, named after a book by Juliana Ewing (see page 106), became 'Open'; they had previously only been for Trull School pupils.

In the early 1970s Rita Sandford, who had herself been a Trull guide, started to assist the Leader, Norma Sankey, and eventually became Leader herself. The photo shows her with the Girl Guides Association Good Service Award, which was presented to her in July 1975 at a monthly Sunday morning Church Parade Service, which was attended by all the uniformed organisations.

Guide Companies were limited to 36, but she remembers that they always had about 40 and sometimes a waiting list. Twice she took a group of about 15 Guides to London for the weekend, including a visit to the theatre. They had to stay at Baden Powell House for Scouts, as the Guide Hostel was not accessible for Rita's wheelchair – the girls enjoyed that arrangement! They also had joint discos with the Scouts in Trull. Rita finally finished as Guide Leader in about 1990. The Guides and Brownies continue to meet weekly in the Pavilion.

Wartime

Both World Wars made a great impact on Trull. Many men volunteered or were conscripted for military service, and refugees, evacuees and servicemen arrived here. Unexpected demands were made on the church. In 1914, a week before Christmas, the vicar was asked to organise a dinner for 150 soldiers at Cotlake! This was a Queen's College Junior boarding house which had presumably been requisitioned for Army use. An appeal was made to parishioners for contributions towards the cost of this, and as usual in Trull the response was impressive. According to the *Parish Magazine* 'an excellent dinner of turkey and plum pudding was provided, along with oranges and cigarettes'.

In January 1915 two cottages at Zaney (now buried beneath the M5 Taunton Deane Services) were furnished for Belgian refugees, who arrived soon afterwards. Local people responded generously to their needs, and a weekly fund was set up to provide food for them.

On 9th January 1919, two months after Armistice Day, a meeting of parishioners was held in the schoolroom to decide how best to commemorate those who had fallen in the Great War. It was decided to erect a war memorial in the south-west corner of the churchyard, giving the names of the 14 men from the parish who had lost their lives, paid for by public subscription. It was unveiled and dedicated on 19th September 1920. Some 25 years later a further five names were added of those who had fallen in the Second World War. The gravestones of those from both wars who are buried in the churchyard were restored by the Commonwealth War Graves Commission to mark the centenary of the end of the Great War in 2018.

During the Second World War, Trull had its own contingent of the Home Guard. The photo shows one platoon, and has kindly been donated to the parish archives by the son of Corporal Prentice (on the left in the back row), who had been in the Machine Gun Corps in the Great War, and was a teacher at Queen's College. The commanding officer was Major Mott. Their

main task seems to have been to guard the filter-beds at Fulwood Pumping Station, on the road to Blagdon Hill, and the reservoirs at Angersleigh. We know about the training they would have been through from the TV series Dad's Army.

On Christmas Day 1940, the services at All Saints included a military parade service attended by 170 Army officers and men from the Sherford Military Camp, where Batt's Park and Queen's Drive are now. They are reported as entering heartily into the worship and thanksgiving. (The old house at Batt's Park had burnt down in 1937, and the site was requisitioned by the War Office on the outbreak of war. It remained as a MoD establishment, latterly as the headquarters of the Army's South Western District, until the present residential development commenced in 1983.)

A week later the Children's Christmas Party was held. Some 160 children assembled in the schoolroom for tea. In spite of rationing the children had a bountiful tea, and afterwards they moved to the Village Hall to be entertained. The reason for the unprecedented number of children was because they included all the evacuee children in the village. Eighty or so children and their teachers came from Ilford and West Ham to escape from the London blitz, and were billeted with local people. Because Trull School was full, some had to be taught in the Parish Room, and the older ones in the Baptist Chapel in Comeytrowe Road where it was found that the younger children could not see over the pews! And a private girls' school from Sussex, Buchanan School, was also evacuated to Trull, and occupied Wild Oak House, at the junction of Wild Oak Lane and Honiton Road. Two huts were erected on Trull Green, as a canteen for evacuee mothers who had accompanied their pre-school children, so they had somewhere to meet. The parish archive includes a number of poignant reminiscences, both by people who had been evacuated here and by local people who had taken them in.

Not all was gloom and doom. 'The sum of nearly £75 was realised for the Red Cross and St John Ambulance Funds as the result of a Garden Fete held at Maryland (now White Lodge) in Dipford Road. The platform, on which the brief opening speeches were made, was decorated with a large V – victory symbol. It was stated at the outset that the proceeds would help supply the needs of the war wounded, prisoners of war, and air raid casualties. Entertainment was given by the pupils of Buchanan School. During the tea interval selections were played by the Buchanan School Percussion Band. Girls from the school led the very successful community singing in the evening. Dancing on the lawns followed at 8pm, when many members of the Forces arrived. Music was supplied by gramophone records'.

Canonsgrove
A regular bus service between Trull and Taunton was in operation by the end of the First World War. In the 1970s it turned into Church Road from Honiton Road, down past the village centre and then up the hill to Brown's Elm, and down Amberd Lane to Staplehay.

Canonsgrove House had become a Police Authority Cadet Training College in 1963, and an accommodation block was built behind it. When the Training College moved to the Police Headquarters at Portishead in 1995, the accommodation became a Hall of Residence for Somerset College of Art and Technology (now Bridgwater and Taunton College), and the bus route was extended to its entrance.

In March 2020, as part of the government's response to the Covid pandemic, all Local Authorities were directed to provide housing for people who were street homeless. In this area the then Somerset West and Taunton Council (working with YMCA Dulverton and the college) placed approximately 50 homeless men and women in one of the unused accommodation blocks at Canonsgrove.

The unplanned introduction of this number of people (many with multiple problems) into a rural environment, with limited support, led to increased reports of antisocial behaviour. Some Trull residents felt frustrated about the lack of consultation and were anxious about the impact of this change of use on the village. In response to these concerns, the Parish Council established a working group, chaired by David Taylor, an independent member of All Saints church, with a mandate to solve problems and restore trust between the parties. This group continued until the homeless project closed in December 2022. Since then, Canonsgrove continues to be used to house medical trainees (both doctors and nurses) and others linked with courses offered by the college.

Trull Sports Club
Trull Sports Club was started in 1920 and for a few years it used Lower Hoges (now King George V Playing Field) as a sports ground. Mr EWA Groves, headmaster of Trull School for 30 years, was Secretary from 1922 until 1949, and one of his first jobs was to find another field. Mrs Bayley of Amberd House kindly let her field Headweir, between the waterfall and Amberd Lane Bridge, rent free to the club, which catered for hockey, football, cricket, putting and tennis. At their AGM in 1929, Trull Sports Club agreed to admit women members, who would play hockey and netball during the winter, and tennis and cricket during the summer. It reached its zenith about 1935. There were two football teams and three hockey teams playing at home and away on Saturdays in winter, as well as three cricket teams in summer playing on the cricket ground in Dipford Road, which Arthur Newton of Dipford House, who was President of the Sports Club and a former Somerset County cricketer, allowed them to use and where they still are more than 100 years later.

The sports club's activities were inevitably largely curtailed during the war years, with many members serving in the armed forces. It revived afterwards, but in 1947 the tennis players decided to form their own club, and moved to the courts in Sweethay Lane where they still are. The other sports could no longer afford the increased rent for Headweir, so gave notice.

The pavilion was donated to the tennis club, cut in half, and moved by lorry! The vicar announced that he had arranged for the footballers to return to Lower Hoges, and 'promised to obtain information from various people re a Playing Field for future use'. The Sports Club was formally disbanded, with its remaining funds donated to Mr Groves in gratitude for all he had done for the Club over so many years.

The football team - or Trull AFC to give it its proper name - continued, and was very strong throughout the 1950s and 1960s. In one famous season they won Division 2 of the Taunton Saturday League and got to two cup finals, winning the first 8-3 and narrowly losing the second 2-1. A great season was celebrated at the Old Village Hall by an end-of-season supper attended by some 150 supporters. The club played in the Trull School colours of green and yellow, and a shirt from the late 1950s was generously donated to the parish archives by Tony Davies, Trull born and bred and an England schoolboy cricketer, who is here displaying it.

Gatchell House Squash and Fitness (later Country) Club

Gatchell House is an early 19th century villa beside the Honiton Road. In 1977 the owner, Derek Hillenbrand, was granted planning permission to build four squash courts adjacent to the Stable block, which was converted to a clubhouse, and the Squash and Fitness Club opened the following year. Facilities included a gymnasium, two all-weather tennis courts, a dance studio (home to the Trull School of Dancing), and a full-size snooker table. It was very popular, and drew members from a wide area.

But 20 years later the site was put on the market and purchased by Somerset Care Trust, and subsequently by Somerset Redstone Trust, with the intention of demolishing the sports facilities and replacing them with supported accommodation for older people. This was bitterly contested by the local Club members, and the design of the first two applications was objected to by Historic England – Gatchell House is in Trull's Conservation Area. But eventually in 2004 planning permission was granted, for a design that properly reflected Trull's vernacular style, and with the proviso that £80,000 be donated towards replacement squash courts (these were eventually provided at the Wyvern Club in Mountfields Road, Taunton).

In 2009 Gatchell Oaks was officially opened. The only relic of the Club is this mural from a 1998 holiday play scheme, that was mounted on the wall of the squash courts. It was rescued shortly before demolition, and can now be seen on the outside wall of the Memorial Hall facing the school playing field.

Women's Institutes

Trull and Staplehay Women's Institute was formed in 1940. One of its most important wartime activities was the organisation of a Fruit Preservation Centre. Over a period of four war years, 56,000 lbs. of jam were made at the jam centre at Quintons in Staplehay, then the home of the founder president Mrs Wells. This was part of the 'Dig for Victory' national campaign to produce as much local food as possible, to compensate for loss of imports and severe rationing. In 1953 the WI won the county-wide competition for a local history – see Preface.

Trull has the distinction of being the only village in Somerset with two Women's Institutes. In November 1952 a second institute was formed, with the name Comeytrowe and District Women's Institute (this was before all the post-war housing had been built in Comeytrowe and Galmington). It held its meetings in the evening, in contrast to the older Institute which met in the afternoons. This was so that every woman, whatever her work, had the opportunity of joining one or the other, and is a distinction that has continued to this day. In 2019 the group changed its name to Trull Trendles WI.

Housing

In the first half of the century, new housing in Trull was confined to single houses, such as those in Honiton Road, Church Road and Wild Oak Lane. After the war, a number of small Council house developments were built - Wyatts Field, Mill Lane and Brookside Close, for example. Then from the 60s onwards, greenfield sites were developed on the fringes of Trull and Staplehay, such as Furlong Green, Patricks Way, Sweethay Close, Spearcey Lane, Barton Green, Amingford Mead and a number of others, all of comparatively small size.

In the short-lived Regional Plan, the South West Regional Spatial Strategy, in the early years of the present century, Taunton was earmarked as a priority for development, on both brownfield and greenfield sites. The fields between Trull and Comeytrowe were seen as a secondary area for urban expansion, after Monkton Heathfield. This was confirmed in the Taunton Deane Local Plan. In 2011, as part of their Localism Act, the government introduced Neighbourhood Plans, which offered local people the opportunity to have more control over planning decisions in their area. A representative group, commissioned by Trull Parish Council and supported by the then Taunton Deane Borough Council, worked on the Plan for three years. The policies and recommendations in the final version, including protected Local Green Space, reflected widespread consultation with local residents and organisations. It was approved at a local referendum and was adopted by the Borough Council in 2017. It was subsequently quoted approvingly by a Government Planning Inspector in his rejection of an appeal against a Borough Council decision to refuse permission to build in Trull Meadow, one of the Local Green Spaces in the Neighbourhood Plan.

Because of the high cost of necessary infrastructure, to deal with problems such as frequent flooding, the Trull and Comeytrowe development was delayed. House building in what became known as Orchard Grove, which can be seen in the distance in the photograph on our front cover, didn't commence until 2022, with the first residents moving in by Christmas. The full development of 2,000 houses is likely to take 10 years to complete.

Orchard Grove Primary School opened in September 2024, as did Orchard Grove Church, using the school facilities every Sunday, led by Revd. John Ball (see photo and final paragraph on p. 36).

Royal celebrations

In 1887, 210 women of Trull contributed £7 5s 6d to the Women's Golden Jubilee Offering to Queen Victoria. Thursday 16th June was observed as the day of Jubilee Commemoration in Trull when: 'The weather was perfect, the service bright and hearty, and the church full. The tent was beautifully decorated, the dinner well served and well cooked, the tea well made, and the sports admirably managed'. The mid-day dinner was for men only, while the tea was for women and children. In 1897 men and women dined together, but otherwise the Diamond Jubilee celebrations were much the same. Jubilee Terrace in Comeytrowe Road was named after Queen Victoria's Diamond Jubilee.

The next record of a royal occasion is of the Coronation of King George V in 1910, when a floral arch was erected in Wild Oak Lane.

The Coronation of Queen Elizabeth II in 1953 was marked by a day of celebrations, as were her Silver and Golden Jubilees. Both were commemorated by a wrought iron gate, into the churchyard from Church Road and beside the Pavilion in the playing field (see photo on page 101). Her Golden Jubilee in 2002 was the occasion of Trull's first 'Party in the Park', which has been subsequently held every other year apart from when Covid intervened. The Queen's Diamond and Platinum Jubilees were also days of celebrations.

A Commemoration Service was held in September 2022 to mark the Queen's death, and the Union Jack was flown at half-mast.

The Coronation of her son, King Charles III, in 2023, was marked by a programme of events, including the church bells to 'Ring for the King', and a 'Picnic in the Park'.

GLOSSARY

accommodation land: land having a special rental value owing to its being required by someone to whom it is let temporarily for the purposes of their business or property.
archdeacon: a member of the clergy having the duty of assisting the diocesan bishop.
benefice: a church office to which an income is attached, usually of a rector or vicar.
bosses: knobs or projections, particularly at the intersection of ribs in a vault.
burgage rents: a fixed monetary annual rent to the landowner, rather than the earlier feudal system of giving service to the manor. 'Burgage' is related to 'borough', where the 'burgesses' (such as merchants and skilled craftsmen), who did not work on the land like the peasantry, held properties from the lord by burgage tenure.
bushel: a unit of volume equal to eight imperial gallons.
c. circa: about the year.
chalice: a cup used to hold the wine at Holy Communion.
chancel: the part of the church containing the altar and seats for the clergy and choir.
chantry: an endowment which supported a chantry priest and a chapel within a church for the celebration of Masses for the souls of the departed.
chapelry: a chapel of ease subordinate to a church elsewhere.
chert: a rock resembling flint and consisting essentially of quartz, found in limestone rather than chalk.
chrismatory: a container for holy oil.
coffer: a chest or strongbox.
combe: a valley or basin.
conventicle: an assembly or meeting of religious dissenters.
cornice: ledge with moulded underside, and the decorative moulding in the angle between wall and ceiling
cross-passage: a passage through a house from front to back.
curate: a member of the clergy serving as an assistant to a rector or vicar. They were formerly often the only priest in a parish, and **perpetual** curates held the living for as long as they wished.
deacon: an assistant to a priest.
demayne (demesne) lands: all the land retained and managed by a lord of the manor under the feudal system for his own use.
double-ogee: a type of moulding, curving first one way then the other.
equestrian dressage: a competition where horse and rider are expected to perform from memory a series of predetermined movements.
evangelical: a movement within Protestant Christianity that emphasizes salvation by faith,

personal conversion, and the authority of Scripture.
fluted pilaster: a column integral with a wall and having a fluted moulding.
freehold of inheritance: land transferable to the owner's successors.
henge: an Early Bronze Age ritual enclosure, usually a ditch with an external bank enclosing a circular flat area.
Henrician: during the reign of King Henry VIII.
hominid: humans, apes and their ancestors.
honorarium: a payment in recognition of services that are nominally given free.
hundreds: units of local government and taxation, intermediate between village and shire. Originally, the term probably referred to a group of 100 hides (units of land required to support one peasant family).
impropriator: a person to whom a benefice is granted as their property.
incumbent: the holder of an Anglican benefice, usually a rector or vicar.
joint benefice: two or more parishes sharing an incumbent but remaining separate parishes.
king-post roof: a roof with a post rising from a tie-beam to the ridge.
kirtle: a woman's long gown or dress.
laths: thin narrow strips of wood, as a support for tiles or plaster.
linhay: a type of two-storey farm building with an open front, with hayloft above and livestock housing below.
manse: the residence of a non-conformist minister.
Mass: the celebration of the service of Holy Communion, especially in Roman Catholic and Anglo-Catholic churches.
messuage: dwelling house with outbuildings and land.
mullions: vertical bars placed between panes of a window.
nucleated: having a concentration of dwellings.
officiant: a priest who presides at Holy Communion or Mass.
ordinance: an authoritative order.
oversailing: projecting.
ovolo: wide convex moulding.
ovoid: shaped like an egg.
palaeoliths: Stone Age tools with points, which could be fixed on to shafts to make spears.
peck: a unit of volume equal to two gallons.
parclose: a parclose screen separates a chapel or an aisle from the rest of the church.
phonograph; an early gramophone.
piscina: a basin for washing Mass vessels, provided with a drain.
polygonal: a two-dimensional figure with three or more straight sides.
post-and-truss: a roof truss in which a tie-beam is supported by a post at each end.

postilion: a person who rides on the nearside leading horse of a team drawing a coach to guide them in the absence of a coachman.
presentment: a statement made on oath by a jury of a matter of fact within their own knowledge.
purlin: a horizontal roof-timber supported by principal rafters and in turn supporting common rafters.
Quadragesima: the first Sunday in Lent.
quoin stones: corner stones.
rator: a person who estimates or determines a rating.
rural dean: a priest supervising one district of a diocese.
scarf-jointed: having two overlapping timbers joined together.
screens passage: a screened-off passage across one end of an open hall.
scroll-stopped: a type of moulding at the end of a chamfered beam.
sestertius: an ancient Roman coin equal to one quarter of a *denarius*.
smoke louvre: a vent to release smoke from the roof of an open hall.
step-stop: another type of moulding at the end of a chamfered beam.
stipend: a fixed sum of money paid to a member of the clergy, as a salary or to meet expenses.
taperer: a person carrying a candle in a religious ceremony.
tithes: a tax of a tenth part of something formerly due in a parish to support its church and priest.
Tithe Apportionment map: an important source of information about the history and topography of a parish, providing details of land ownership and occupation. They were produced in order to assess the tithe payable in cash to the parish church for the support of the church and its clergy.
tracery: openwork pattern of masonry or timber in the upper part of an opening.
trefoil head: the top of an opening or recess, having three lobes.
vernacular architecture: concerned with domestic and functional rather than public or monumental buildings.
visitation: visit of inspection by an archdeacon.
wind-brace: a curving roof timber under the slope of a roof.

INDEX

Aberdeen, Scotland 107
Acland 7
Act of Uniformity 32, 61
Adam, Andy 15
Aethelwulf, King 4
Algar of Sernege 82
All Saints Church iii, v, 36, 37, 47, 101, 104, 140
　see also Trull Church
All Saints Parish 5
Allen, Mrs Jefferys 97
Allen, Reverend William Jefferys 70
Allen, William Jefferys JP 33
Amberd Bridge 136
Amberd Farmhouse 25
Amberd House 26, 111, 130, 140
Amberd Lane 2, 61, 88, 130, 139, 140
Amery, Mary 80
Amingford Grange 9,
Amingford Mead 66, 130, 143
Angersleigh 34, 36, 37, 69, 72, 80, 84, 133, 139
Anne, Queen 53
Antioch, Turkey 41
Archbishop of Canterbury 51
Archdeacon of Taunton 53
Archer, Don ii, 47
Archer, JW 42
Ascot, Berkshire 92
Ash Priors 44
Ashe Farm 14
Atton, Mr 54
Atwood, George 33
Aurelius, Marcus 1
Australia 34
Avery, WH 79

Babb, Edward 63
Babb, John 59, 79
Babb, Thomas 32
Babbe, Ede 49, 57
Babbe, family 49, 57

Badcock, Henry Jefferies 70
Baden-Powell, Agnes 137
Baden-Powell, Robert 136, 137
Baden-Powells 106
Baker, John 7, 59, 68, 83, 84
Baker, John jnr 83, 84
Bakker, Paddy 118
Ball, Elizabeth 32
Ball, John 32
Ball, Rev Imogen 36
Ball, Jon 36, 144
Ball, William 31
Ballard, Richard Ernest 34, 35
Band of Hope 97, 110
Baptist Chapel, Comeytrowe Road 98, 113, 139
Baptist Union Corporation 112, 114
Barbados 61
Barklett, Thomas 59
Barnicott, James 103
Barrett, Major Alexander Gould 125
Barton Estate 29, 49
Barton Grange 68
Barton Green 94, 143
Bathpool 88, 89
Bathpool Mill 51
Batts 69
Batts Farm 15, 16
Batts House 69, 110
Batts Park 16, 69, 110
Bayley, Harry 68
Baylis, Harry 32
Bayly, John 32
Bayly, Mrs 130, 140
Bell House 111
Beny, John 48
Bere, Humphrey 49
Berrie, Edward 45
Berry, Benjamin 32, 60, 61
Beverage, Nancy 127
Bevis, John 87

~ Index ~

Bevis, Thomas 75
Bicknell, family 23
Bicknell, Isaac 79
Bicknell, Reuben 92
Bicknell, Susannah 92
Billets, Samuel 54
Birchall, Arthur 104
Bishop of Bath and Wells 29, 68, 124, 129
Bishop of Winchester 72, 82
Bishops Hull 10, 49, 53, 68, 75, 89
Bisson, Geoff viii
Blagdon Hill 117, 136, 139
Blake, family 80, 83
Blake, John 59
Blake, Margaret 83
Blake, Richard 79
Blake, Robert 60, 79
Blake, Thomas 70, 80, 81
Blake, William 46, 80, 86
Blanket Club 110
Bloody Assizes 61
Bloxham, Barry 128, 130
Bond, Sir George vi
Bonsey, Revd Richard Yerburgh 34, 35, 116
Borough of Taunton 5
Bour, Jone 57
Bowerman family 119, 121
Boxenhedge 22, 30, 92, 122
Boxenhedge Farm 133
Boxenhedge Green 133
Bridgwater 79, 135
Bridgwater and Taunton College 140
Britton, Mr 98
Broadlands, Staplehay 2
Broadmead, Mrs Elizabeth vi
Bromwich, David vii
Brookside Close 9, 66, 143
Broomfield 45
Brown, F 54
Brown, John 31
Brown's Elm 5, 61, 139
Brownies 106, 137
Browning, Mr 122
Bryan, Sir Francis 30

Bryceson, Mr H 44
Buces 92
Buchanan School, Sussex 139
Budleigh Farms 72-74
Bull, Albert 116
Bull, John 52, 53
Bull, Thomas 52
Buncombe, family 21, 70, 83
Buncombe, John 70, 71, 101
Buncombe, Thomas 84
Buncombe, William 7, 59
Burge, Ken vii, 126, 127
Burlescombe, Mid Devon 77
Burrough, Andrew 74
Burroughs, family 79
Burrow Mump, Burrowbridge 125
Bus service 139
Bush, RJE 6, 47, 54
Butler, Charles 85
Butler, Patrick 85
Bynny, John 48

Cade, James 79
Cade, John 57
Cade, Robert 57
Calamy, Edmund 62
Caldecott, Randolph 106
Cambridge 104
Cann, George 79
Canonsgrove 7, 78, 79, 139, 140
Canonsgrove Farm 74, 79
Canonsgrove Farmhouse 79
Canonsgrove House 111, 140
Carter's Orchard 111
Castle House, Taunton Castle 103
Castleman's Hill 2, 74, 75
Census returns 7, 115, 120. 121
Chandos Brass Ensemble 127
Chantry Cottage 16, 29, 46, 70
Chard, John VC 125
Charles I, King 60
Charles II, King 60, 61
Charles III, King 145
Chilcott, John 122

150

~ Index ~

Chilliswood Farm 2, 12, 30, 42, 76, 77, 84, 94, 122
Chipchase, Nick viii, 134
Christchurch, Cockfosters, North London 36
Church benchends 40
Church House, Trull 42, 45, 46, 48, 50, 52, 55, 96, 123, 124
Church of England National Society 101
Church Office, Trull 106
Church Parade Service 137
Church Road, Trull ii, 15, 111, 115-117, 119, 122, 139, 143, 145
Church seating plans 7, 34, 39
Churchill, Sir Winston vi
Churchyard see Trull Churchyard
Civil War vi, 59, 60, 62
Clapp, Francis John 33
Claremont 5, 9, 111
Clatworthy family 80, 81, 83
Clerk's Cottage 16, 29
Cliffe, LA 33
Clitsome, John 33
Close, Mark 36
Cob Garden 69
Cockshayes Green 69, 132
Cogan, William 59
Coke, John 31
Coles, widow 69
Collard, Michael 116
College Chapel see Queen's College Chapel
Colles, Humphrey 29, 49
Collinson vi
Collis, Ivor 20
Coltehirste, Matthew 30
Comeytrowe 3, 70, 86, 112, 143
Comeytrowe Lane 97, 113
Comeytrowe Parish 6
Comeytrowe Road 5, 98, 113, 139, 144
Common land 133
Commonwealth War Graves Commission 138
Community Council for Somerset 66
Community Infrastructure Levy 131
Convalescent Hospital, Highgate, London 107
Cooper, Lady 30
Coplestons 9, 111

Coram, Mr 80
Corder, Alan 73
Corder, Heather 73
Corfe 49, 113, 114, 132
Corner, Elizabeth 80
Corner, Mary 80
Cotlake 137
Cotlake Hill 1, 2
Cottle family 63, 64
Cox, John 72
Cox, Neville 37
Coxe's 77, 110
Coxes Farm 94
Crane, Mrs Rosemary 127
Cranmer, John 20
Cricket Club 131
Criddle, Debbie 117
Cridge, JT 92
Cridland, Frauncis 59
Crippen, TG 114
Cromwell, Oliver 60
Cromwell, Richard 60
Crosse, John 68, 75
Crowcombe 123
Crown Inn 119, 120, 125, 136
Crudge, Debbie viii
Cruikshank, George 106
Culmstock, Devon 76
Cutliffe Farm 86
Cutsey (Farm) 2, 70, 79-81, 83, 86, 87
Cutsey House 80, 81

Dare, Richard 59
Davey, George 83
David, Gerald 116
Davies, Tony 141
Daw's Green 80, 110, 112, 122, 133
Daw's Green Cottage 77
Dawe, William 92
Day family 115, 116
Day, Samuel 85
de Lym, Master Simon 29, 49
de Sorewella, Willelmus 10
Deane Drive 5

151

~ Index ~

Dedman, Simon 119
Dedman, Tim 119
deGex, Victor 73
Denbaud, William 32
Denewulf, Bishop of Winchester 4
Dening, Miss Amy 109
Denning, Benjamin 70
Denning, Edwin 97
Denning, Kate 97
Dept. of Education & Science 125
Derbie, Roger 32
Derrick, W viii
Devon 12, 38, 60, 76
Dickson, Michael 33
Dight, Anne 59
Dipford (Dupeforde) Tithing 76
Dipford 4, 5, 30, 33
Dipford Farm 19
Dipford House 8, 80, 140
Dipford Orchard 9, 66
Dipford Road 20, 122, 131-133, 139, 140
Doble and Shire 132
Doble, Arthur 119
Doble, Mr 122
Doble, Samuel 16
Domesday Book 10
Domet family 72
Dommett, William 59
Done, Miss 92
Dorset 61
Dragon Bookshop, Taunton iv
Drew, Mr 126
Duke of Monmouth 75
Dulverton 61, 140
Dunning, Robert W vii, 7, 9, 11, 18, 47, 54, 62
Dunster 12
Durston, George 59
Dusgate, G viii
Dymond, John 76

East Anglia 38
East Reach, Taunton 68
Eastbrook 5, 7, 79, 86, 112, 122, 135
Eastbrook Estate 26

Eastbrook House 26, 96, 111
Eastbrook Lodge 111
Edward the Elder, King 4
Edward VI, King 44, 50, 67
Edward VII, King 97
Edwards, John 62
Edwards, Sarah 62
Edwards, Robert 59
Eeles, Dr FC 52
Eggins, Richard 81
Eggins, Ruth 81
Ekwall, E 6
Eley, Mr vii
Eley, Mrs S vii
Elphinstone, William Harry 97
Elizabeth I, Queen 52, 55-57
Elizabeth II, Queen 101, 130, 145
Emerson, Major General 15
England, Colonel 15
Evacuees 113, 124, 137
Evans, Revd Derek Courtney 34, 35, 126
Everett, Tim 73
Ewing, Alexander 106, 137
Ewing, Juliana 106, 137

Fairlawn Coach House 122
Fairview Terrace 111
Farmer, John 55
Farthings 72
Fayrwyll, Simon 49
Fideoak Slaughter House, Bishops Hull 89
Finberg, HPR 6
Flanders 51
Flooding 135, 143
Fons S George, Wilton 29
Forde, John 67
Fouracre, family 112
Fouracre, G and Sons 122
Fouracre, Martin 88
Foy, Robert 23
French, family viii, 70, 79, 87-89, 122
French, William 103
Frene, John 31
Friends' Meeting House, Taunton 77

152

~ Index ~

Frithogyth, Queen 4
Fry, CG 129
Fugers, Lieutenant 59
Fuljames, Anthony 30
Fullards Farm 74, 79
Fulwood Independent chapel 112, 114
Fulwood Pumping Station 139
Furlong Green 9, 143

Gadd, Thomas 83
Gale, John 33
Gale, Mrs 83
Galmington 30, 67, 114, 142
Galmington Youth Centre 114
Gardner, Christopher 59
Gardner, Valentine 59
Gatchell Cottage 12, 20
Gatchell House 8, 22, 33, 70, 97, 111, 141
Gatchell Oaks 9, 66, 111, 142
Gatchell Spinney 20, 21
Gatchell, Thomas 79
Gatchell, Mrs 79
Gaylard, George 61
Gaylard, Meller 61
Geb, Jon 33
Gebons, Cristofer 57
Gebons, Hary 57
Gensum, Joan 57
Geoff Hewett Pavilion 94, 136, 145
George Rosewell, George 59
George V, King 98, 126, 127, 144
George V Playing Field see Playing Field
Georges Farm, 76, 80
Giffard, William, Bishop of Winchester 5
Gifford, John 124
Gill, John 59
Gillo, R viii
Gilson, Ron 26, 27
Girl Guides 106, 137
Glencoe Terrace 111, 122
Glossary 146
Goodenough, Smart 30
Gould, Robert John 33
Govier, Burnett 136

Govier, family 112
Graham, Steve 127
Granger, Copetone 59
Grant, family 84
Grant, Graham ii
Great Liscombe 69
Green, Cyril W ii, v, vii, 15, 16, 18, 20, 22-24, 26, 28, 36, 45, 47, 87, 90, 96, 101, 111
Green, Roger Lancelyn 106
Greenslade, family, 23
Greenslade, Richard, 70
Groves, EW 98
Groves, Mr EWA 140, 141
Grundy, JB 6
Gybbbens, Jone 57

Haines Hill 9
Halcon, Taunton 113
Hall, Mr 78
Hallam, AD iv
Hallam, Olive ii, iv
Ham Hill, Stoke-sub-Hamdon 37
Hamatt Wood 83
Hamilton, John 83
Hamwood (Hamwode) 12, 29, 75, 77, 82-84, 86, 90
Hancock, Rt Revd Peter 130
Handy Shop 117
Hankridge Arms 14
Harding, Tony 28
Harman, Sarah 96
Harness, Dr 15
Harness, Thomas Burnaford 70
Harpers 79
Harries, Christopher 95
Harris, John 32, 59
Harvey, John 32
Haskoll, Rev Farnham 95
Hathway, Ross 34, 35
Hawkings, brothers 77
Hawkings, family 90
Hawkings, Miss 84
Hawkins, family 81
Hawkyns, William 49

~ Index ~

Hayes, George 109, 116
Hayes, James 32
Haygrove 15, 16
Haygrove Farm 16, 135
Haygrove Farmhouse 16
Haygrove House 16
Hayne, Phillip 59
Haynysworthe, John 16
Hazeldene 115, 116
Headteacher's Office, Trull 100
Headweir 130, 140
Hedderwick, David 91
Hedderwick, Maria 91
Heidelberg, Germany 107
Heliar, John 52
Helyar, Revd Hugh 92
Helyar, Vivian 86, 89
Hemyock, Devon 34
Henrico de Cuttleshegh 79
Henry VIII, King 30, 48
Henson family 77, 78
Herswell Farm 30, 75
Heryng family 53, 55, 56, 72
Hewett, family 90, 94
Hewett, Geoff 131
Hewett, James 77
Hewett, Mary 77
Hewett, Thomas 109
Hewitt, Miss 114
Hewsey, John 32
High Path 15
Higher Canonsgrove 79
Higher Comeytrowe 2
Higher Dipford 89
Higher Kibbear 85
Higher Longcroft 30
Higher Sweethay (Farm) 87, 89-91, 94
Hill, Roger 72
Hillbrook House 8
Hillenbrand, Derek 141
Hillside Cottage 16
Hillside Farm 16
Hine, John 79
Hine, Susan 79
Hine, Thomas 92
Hippo, Algeria 39
Holway 82
Holway, Hundred of 76
Home Guard 138
Homeless accommodation 140
Hong Kong 94
Honiton Road 110, 111, 116, 117, 132, 139, 141, 143
Horte, Thomas 59
Housing 5, 15, 36, 50, 65, 66, 70, 89, 96, 105, 111, 134, 136, 140, 142, 143
Housing Act 65, 66
Hughes, Mr 92
Hughes, Mrs RA 92
Hughes, Shirley vii
Hull, Hundred of 5, 76
Hull, John 52
Hulland, Mr Edmund 127
Hurlbatt, Cdr Jeremy RN viii, 87
Hurly, James 33
Hurly, James jnr 33
Hurrell, Simon 127

Ilchester 64
Ilford, Greater London 98, 139
Infant Clinic 132
James I, King 13, 14
Jansum, Joan 57
Jeans, Sarah viii, 28
Jeboult, Edward 45, 123
Jeffreys, Judge 61
Jenkins, John 20
Joanne de Cuttleshegh 79
Jones Gisperus 31
Jones, Edward 117
Jones, Elizabeth 117
Jones, Fitzroy 63, 65, 66
Jones, Joan 117
Jones, Margaret 100
Jubilee Terrace 144
Just Hair 117

~ Index ~

Kebby, John 45
Keene, Edward 83
Keene, Elizabeth 20
Keene, Thomas 20, 31, 38
Keene, Thomas jnr 20
Kelly's County Directory 115
Kene, Anthony 31, 53
Kene, Joan or Jone 39
Kene, Thomas 56
Kerr, Miss Deborah 125
Kerr-Pearse, Revd Beauchamp 16
Kibbear 5, 7, 79, 84, 85
Kibbear Cottages 24
Kibbear Farm 23, 85, 86
Kibbear Farmhouse 86
Kibbear House 84
Kibbear Lane 86
Kien, Joan or Jone 39
Killams 6
Killams Green 6
Killarney, County Kerry 107
King George V Playing Field see Playing Field
King, William 59
King's Gatchell 13, 14, 19, 70, 124
Kipling, Rudyard 106
Kirke, Colonel 61
Knight Garden 69
Knight House 69
Knight, Thomas 69

Lady Land or Ladyland 46, 50, 69, 70
Lady Liscombe (The Parish Field) 69, 70
Ladylawn 70
Lambe, Christian 57
Lane, John 45
Lane, Mr 109
Lanne, Crysten 57
Lawrence, Mr EO 114
Leamon, Anne viii, 122
Leamon, Robin viii, 122
Lee, Mr George JP 126
Lehner, Andy 130, 131
Lentall, Mr 122
Lethbridge, Ambrose 96

Lilac Cottages 15, 122
Lillington, Frederick 33
Lipe Hill 80
Liscombe 50, 69, 70
Liscombe Mead 69
Little Canonsgrove 26
Little Hamwood 83
Local Plan 66, 143
Lock, brothers 122
Lock, family 90, 92
Lock, Les viii
Lome, Hughe 52
London 15, 30, 36, 60, 61, 85, 97, 137
London University vii, 104
Long Sutton 81
Loosemore, Samuel 120
Lord, Mr viii
Lord, Mrs P viii
Loughborough Foundry, Leicestershire 47
Lower Canonsgrove 78, 85
Lower Comeytrowe 30
Lower Comeytrowe Farm 97
Lower Gatchell 14
Lower Hoges 95, 127, 140
Lower Longcroft 30
Lower Sweethay (Farm) 28, 91, 92
Lower Sweethay Farmhouse 91
Lowe-Smith, M viii
Lowton (Louton) 53, 68
Lucrese Keen, 59
Luke, family 117
Luscombe 49,
Lynas, Arnold 135

M5 (Taunton Deane) Services 83, 86, 138
M5 motorway 2, 6, 81, 86
Magdalene Hall, Oxford 60
Manor of Taunton Deane 4, 5, 10, 20, 67, 69, 70, 72, 84, 120
Map of Trull Parish 6
Marke, Theophilus Tripe 71
Marks, David vii 109, 131, 136
Marlborough, Duke of vi
Marston, Mr FW 126

~ Index ~

Mary Land (Maryland), USA 62,
Maryland 139
Mary Tudor, Queen 50
Mason, William 77
Matthews FW 74
Matthews, AG 62
Matthews, George 20
Matthias, Neil 116
Mattock, Reuben 72, 78
Mattock, Robert 20, 44, 72
Mattock, Susannah 20
Mayberry, Tom vii, 3, 6, 42, 62
Mayled, Nick 119
McDermott, Mark B ii, v, 16, 18, 20, 28, 47, 54
McDonald, Pat 33
McKinley, Luke 87
Melverton see Milverton
Membury, S 6
Memorial Hall 125-128, 130, 142
Men's Club 98, 124, 127
Men's Club Hall see New Men's Club
Merthyr, Rt. Hon. Lord 126
Methodist Independent Schools Trust 104
Middle Sweethay (Farm) viii, 27, 28, 87, 90, 91, 92
Middle Sweethay Farmhouse 91
Middleton, William 85
Mill Lane 4, 65, 66, 122, 135, 143
Mill Pond 16
Mill see Water mill
Milligan, Ted 99, 117
Milverton (Melverton) 53
Minehead 116
Ministers' Accounts 29
Mission Room 80
Mo, Thomas 59
Moggridge family 61
Monkton Heathfield 143
Monmouth, Duke of 61
Moore, John 59
Moore, Thomas 59
More Close 30
Mott, Major 138
Mountbatten Nursing Home 106
Mountfields Road, Taunton 116, 141

National Health Service 132
National Playing Field Foundation 137
National Trust 125
Naughton, Martine vii
Neal, Vivian 75
Nesbit, E 106
New Barn Park 5
New Men's Club (and Parish Room) 124, 127
New Rectory 127
New Vicarage 116
Newley Farm 75
Newton, Arthur 140
Newton, Francis Milner 30
Newton, Josepha Sophia 30
Nicholas of Chiliwordiswode 76
Nicholl, Major 26
Nicholl, Mrs 26
Norman, Caroline 46, 71
Norman, Chris 1, 3
North Curry 94
North Trendle 5
North Trendle Tithing 55, 69, 70, 72, 93
Nycolas the organ maker 48

Oakfield Terrace 111
Old Music Room, Queen's College 103
Old Rectory 2, 34
Old Vicarage 33, 34, 116
Old Village Hall 98, 102, 124, 125, 128, 129, 139, 141
Orbach, Julian 84, 94
Orchard Close 15
Orchard Grove 3, 6, 131, 143
Osborne, Dinah 85
Osborne, family, 78
Osborne, GE 92
Our Lady's House 49, 68
Overseers of the poor 63, 64, 76
Owl Garage 119
Owsley, William 68
Oxford 104

Paget, Mrs Byng 41
Palmer, Basil 79

156

~ Index ~

Palmer, FH 79
Palmer, William vi, 50, 67
Parish Archive(s) & Group ii, v, 16, 28, 45, 59, 102, 106, 109, 121, 125, 138, 139, 141
Parish Magazine vii, 34, 83, 110, 115, 121, 127, 131, 136, 138
Parish Nurse 132
Parish Room(s) 45, 98, 100, 123-125, 128, 129, 132, 136, 137, 139
Park Close 9
Parkinson Society 106
Parkinson, John 106
Parnell, John 32
Parochial Church Council 5, 128, 129
Parris family 86, 92
Parris, Georgina viii
Parris, Peter 79
Parry Jones, Dr 20
Parry Jones, Mrs 20
Party in the Park 145
Passmore, Miss May Ann 109
Patricks Way 143
Pavilion see Geoff Hewett Pavilion
Pearce Suite 127
Pearce, Messrs 127
Pears, Roberte 56
Pearson, Colonel 68
Penny, Richard 46
Penny, Thomas 112, 113
Penoyre, Jane 14, 15
Penoyre, John 14, 15
Peston, William 31
Pevsner, Nikolaus 39, 47, 94
Pewtress, Ruth 47
Philip of Cochage 11
Philips, Cherry 118
Philips, Sandra 118
Phillips, Nathaniell 59
Phillypps, Anthony 48, 49
Phyllis, Sister 113, 114
Pidgeon, Julian 82
Pilates Studio 116, 117
Pitminster 2, 4-7, 9-11, 27, 29, 34, 49, 60, 61, 67-69, 87, 94, 97, 112, 115, 132, 134

Playing field (King George V) 94, 95, 100, 101, 127, 130, 131, 140
Playing Field (School) 142
Polwheel, Elizabeth 60
Pook Lane 124
Pool Room 99
Poole, Charles 85
Poole, Mr 84
Poor Houses 46, 65, 69, 70
Porlock 12
Porter, family 87
Portishead 140
Post Box 117
Post Office iv, 116, 117, 118
Potter, George 52
Poundisford (Pundlesforda) 5, 11, 60, 78, 89, 95, 134
Poundisford Lodge 86
Poundisford Park 2, 44
Powell, Lt. Col. 59, 83
Pratt, Miss Ann 109
Pratt, Miss Sarah 109
Prentice, Corporal 138
Price, George 59
Priest, Peter 30
Prieste, William 51
Pring, Dr Daniel 23
Prior of Taunton Priory 29, 49
Prior, John Miskin 34, 35
Prior, Phyliss 34, 35
Priorswood School, Taunton 99
Pritchard, Mark 124
Provident Club 110
Prowse, Thomas 64
Pulman, Christopher 52
Puriton 79
Purvis, Dr 77
Pytmyster see Pitminster

QEII Field 130
Queen's College iii, 34, 103-105, 133, 137, 138
Queen's Drive 50, 139
Queen's Junior School 104
Quintons 111, 142

Rackhouse 77
Ralph, Colin viii, 79
Rats' Castle 136
Ray, Mr 54
Ray, Rev Richard 104
Reaphay 80, 86, 87
Reaphay Farm 87
Reaphay Farm Cottages viii
Rectory, Farm of 29
Red Tiles 110
Reformation 29, 44, 48, 49, 50, 67
Refugees 83, 137, 138
Richard of Buddlegh 72
Richard, Bishop of Bath and Wells 68
Richards, Mr 117
Richards, Mrs 117
Ridwood, Betty 64
Rixham Mead 49, 68, 70
Roach, Mervyn 133
Roach, Virginia 133
Robert of Depeforda 11
Roberts, Sid 126
Roffe-Silvester, family 87
Rose Cottage 120
Rose, Susan viii
Rosewell, Maurice 87
Rosewell, William 87
Rowsewell, Thomas 57
Royal Bath and West Show 137
Royal celebrations 144
Rumwell 37, 75
Rumwell Hall 75
Rumwell Manor 37, 75
Rumwell Quarry 75
Rural Dean 34, 148

Sabyn, John 31, 48, 49, 57
St Ambrose 39
St Andrew's Plymouth 36
St Augustine of Hippo 39
St George 41
St George's Church, Wilton 5
St Gregory 39
St James' Baths, Taunton 99

St Jerome 39
St John the Evangelist 39
St Margaret of Antioch 41
St Mary Magdalene's Church, Taunton 29, 34
St Michael 41
Salisbury Plain 124
Sanders, Robert 59
Sandford, Rita 137
Sankey, Norma 137
Scouts vii, 136, 137
Sedgemoor, battle of 61
Seller, Rev Henry James 33, 109
Selwood, John 64
Semson, Roger 44
Sernage (Zaney) 82-84, 138
Sharpe, David viii, 104
Sharpe, John 31
Sherford Military Camp 139
Sherford Stream (Scitere) 4, 16, 135, 136
Sherford, William 59
Sherwood, William 82
Shire family 118, 119
Shut, John 52
Silver Street Baptist Church 112, 114
Singapore 94
Siraut, Mary vii
Skinner, Richard 83, 93
Small, Harold 24, 85, 86
Smart, Mr PW 114
Smith, Foull, 53
Smith, John 67
Smith, Revd LJ Egerton 113, 114
Smith, Susannah 84, 85
Smith, William 67
Smyth, Henry 82
Smyth, John 67, 83
Smythe, Robarte 48
Solway, Evelyn v, 61, 62
Somer Lease (Summer Leaze) 30
Somerset 4, 9, 12, 38, 54, 57, 60, 61, 63, 64, 74, 80, 84, 123, 125, 142
Somerset Archaeological & Natural History Society viii
Somerset Avenue, Taunton 5

Somerset College of Art and Technology 140
Somerset County Council vii, 3, 6, 11, 15, 62, 94, 101, 125
Somerset County Gazette vii, viii, 77, 104, 136
Somerset Heritage Centre vii, 50, 96, 123
Somerset Historic Environment Record vii, 1, 3
Somerset Museum 44
Somerset Playing Field Association 127
Somerset West and Taunton Council 140
South Trendle (Southtrendle) 5, 7
South View Terrace 111
South West Heritage Trust viii, 3
South West Regional Spatial Strategy 143
Southam, John Henry 34
Southay see Southwell
Southwell (once Southay) 9
Southwell Lodge 111
Southwick House 14, 70
Southwood, Thomas 68, 69, 72
Sparks family 84
Sparks, Mark 26
Spaxton 88
Spearcey 79, 87-89
Spearcey Close 118
Spearcey Farm 78, 87-89
Spearcey Lane 143
Spiller family 24, 85
Spiller, Alan 88
Spiller, Jesse 97
Spy Post House 111
Squibb, Mr 32
Stamp, Harold William Tremlett 34, 35
Stanbury, Charles 84
Stansell, William 44
Staplegrove 10
Staplehay 2, 5, 7, 9, 16, 87, 99, 112, 118-120, 122, 125, 136, 139, 142, 143
Staplehay Auto Services 120
Staplehay Stores 118
Staplehay Weir 4, 16
Stawell, Sir John 59, 60
Steart 73, 79, 80, 82
Steart Barn 81, 82
Steart Cottages 82

Steele, Mark 73
Steele, Sue 73
Stephens, John 69, 92
Stephens, Sarah 69, 92
Stevens, Robert 59
Stibbs, John 33
Stocks 46, 80, 107
Stone House 69
Strickland, Edward 20
Strickland, Jane 20
Strickland, Joseph 20
Stroud, Francis 62
Stroud, Justine 62
Stuckey, Mr 54
Sturge 7
Stutt, Christopher 92
Sussex 139
Sweep, Henry 70
Sweethay Close 9,
Sweethay Court viii, 27, 84, 87, 89-91
Sweethay Lane 91, 140
Sweethay Studio 118
Sweethay viii, 7, 27, 88, 90
Sykes, Elizabeth 84

Taunton Carnival 137
Taunton Castle 5, 11, 61, 103, 104
Taunton Deane Borough Council & Local Plan 66, 143
Taunton Deane Borough Council & planning applications 3
Taunton Deane Enclosure Act (1851) 133
Taunton Deane Planning Authority 130
Taunton Deane, Manor of: see Manor of Taunton Deane
Taunton ii, iv, 3-5, 9, 10, 30, 49, 53, 59-61, 68, 77, 80, 97-99, 112, 115, 116, 118, 134-136, 139, 141, 143
Taunton Market 88
Taunton Minster 29
Taunton Parish 6, 70, 131
Taunton Priory 5, 6, 29, 49, 82
Taunton Rural District Council 66, 125
Taunton Turnpike Trust 110

Taunton, Borough of 5
Taunton, Monastery of 29
Taylor, Dave 28
Taylor, David 140
Teale, Kenneth William Pridgin 34
Temperance Movement 34, 110
Temple Methodist Church, Taunton 104, 105
Tennis Club 141
Terndrup, Mrs 117
Thatched Cottage 116
The Corner Shop 118
The Lawn 9
Thomas, Botolph 83
Thomas, family 72
Thomas, John 7, 68
Thomas, Ysbell 57
Thornfalcon 14
Threadneedle Street, City of London 85
Three Corners 133
Tickner, Ron 127
Tinning, Keith 90
Tithings v
Topsham 61
Totterdell's Farm 54
Toy, Clem 46
Trendle (Trendele, Trindele) 4, 10, 11, 29, 76, 82
Trevelyan, George 41
Trevelyan, Prebendary Charles William 34, 35, 127
Trood family 87, 90
Trood, John 78
Trout, Thomas 46
Trull (Trulle) vi, vii, 1-10, 12, 27-31, 34, 41, 44, 45, 48, 49, 53, 57-72, 75-77, 81, 83, 86, 87, 94-97, 99, 100, 105, 106, 109-115, 117, 123, 125, 126, 128, 129, 132-144
Trull Acre 68
Trull Action Plan Group 128
Trull AFC 141
Trull Allotments Association 125
Trull Chapel 113, 114
Trull Church Community Centre ii, v, 98, 102, 106, 122, 136
Trull Church see also All Saints Church 29, 42, 55, 56, 75, 83, 84, 90, 93, 104, 105, 108, 144

Trull Churchyard 4, 16, 29, 42, 45-48, 50, 52, 54, 55, 65, 69, 96, 107, 123, 136, 138, 144
Trull Community Centre Development Group 128
Trull Cricket Club 131
Trull Garage 119, 132
Trull Green 66, 68, 69, 94, 109, 116, 119, 132, 133, 139
Trull Green Drive 9
Trull Green Farm 92, 94, 131
Trull Lands 68
Trull Meadow 4, 16, 105, 126, 133, 135, 143
Trull Moor 30, 71
Trull Museum 121
Trull Neighbourhood Plan 134
Trull Parish Council v, 5, 66, 70, 79, 126, 130, 134, 143
Trull Parish Lands Charity & Community Fund 50, 67, 68, 102, 125
Trull Parish Plan 128
Trull Pre-School 102
Trull Road 103, 106, 110
Trull School vii, 16, 18-20, 22-24, 26, 28, 34, 36, 70, 71, 85, 96, 99, 101, 102, 113, 126, 131, 134, 137, 139-141
Trull Sports Club vii, 130, 140
Trull Stores 116, 117, 119
Trull's Pavilion, 131
Tucker, George 59
Tucker, James 69
Tudball, Thomas 33

Union Workhouse, Trinity Road, Taunton 65
Upper Canonsgrove 78
Upper Hoges 66, 95

Vale of Taunton 62
Valor Ecclesiasticus 29, 31, 49
Venn, family 75, 76
Venn, Mr viii
Venn, Mrs W viii
Venn, Mr 122
Vibart, Commander James RN 77
Vibart, family 42

~ Index ~

Vicarage 49, 132
Victoria, Queen 44, 54, 103, 109, 144
Villa Ponente 106
Village Hall see Old Village Hall
Vilven, Thomas 63
Vine Cottage 15, 18, 19
Virgin Mary 44, 46, 48, 67
Virginia, USA 62
Vivary green wedge 130
Voysey, William 67

Wadsworth, Andrew 36
Wakefield, Mr 136
Wallace, Mark 36
War Memorial 96, 136, 138
Warman, Simon 40, 41
Wartime 137, 142
Water mill 16
Watson, John 80
Watts family 75
Waye, John 40, 41
Weaver, FW 54
Webb, Adrian viii, 62
Webber, Cyril 75
Webster, Chris vii, 3
Welch, Shirley vii, viii
Welcome Home Committee 125
Wellington 84
Wellington Road 68
Wells 65, 68
Wells Cathedral 48, 57
Wells Cathedral School 34
Wells, Mrs 142
Welman, Isaac 95
Welman, Simon 95
Welman, Thomas 95
West Buckland 20, 80
West Ham, East London 98, 139
West Hatch 87
West of England Developments Ltd 138
West, Gilbert H 33
Westcott, Mr 54
Weston Zoyland 61
Wetham, James 83

Whale, Harry 85, 96, 97, 100
Whale, Mr 15, 134
Wheat, Colonel 30
Whitchurch, Devon 60
White Lodge 9, 139
White, Frederick 87, 90
White, James 23
Whithorne, Thomas 45
Whyte, Robert 31
Wigram, Miss 15, 124, 129
Wild Oak 8
Wild Oak Lane 2, 16, 70, 110, 111, 116, 127, 143, 144
Wild Oak House 139
William of Reaphegh 86
William of Swafam 11
Williams, Cdr EHD 15, 17-19, 21, 22, 24-26, 28, 74
Wilton 10, 29
Wilton Church 5, 129
Winchester Arms 4, 120, 135
Winchester Cathedral 4
Winchester, Bishop of 62
Winterton, Revd Martin Leonard 34-36, 38, 47, 124
Wolland, Roger 59
Women's Institutes iv, 73, 142
Wood family 59, 76
Woodberry, John 85
Woodford, Mr SB 114
Woodland (Tithing) 5, 69, 82
Woodland, John 55
World War I 103, 121, 139
World War II 85, 98, 113, 117, 125, 138
Wrangrove (or Wrantmore), Betsy 96
Wyatt, Henry 59
Wyatt, John 46, 70, 95, 123, 127
Wyatt, Mr 68
Wyatt, Prudence 95, 123
Wyatts Field 9, 66, 96, 110, 143
Wylkyns, Raffe 31

Yarcombe, Devon 79
Yordeyn, John 49

Youings, Rev Adrian 36, 129

Zaney (Sernage) 82-84, 138

www.ingramcontent.com/pod-product-compliance
Lightning Source LLC
Chambersburg PA
CBHW051315110526
44590CB00031B/4365